T0128339

ADVICE FROM A YOGI

◆ ◆ ◆

ADVICE FROM A YOGI

*An Explanation of a Tibetan Classic
on What Is Most Important*

KHENCHEN THRANGU

◆ ◆ ◆

PADAMPA SANGYE'S
One Hundred Verses

◆ ◆ ◆

Translated by the
THRANGU DHARMAKARA
TRANSLATION COLLABORATIVE

SHAMBHALA
Boulder
2015

Sʜᴀᴍʙʜᴀʟᴀ Pᴜʙʟɪᴄᴀᴛɪᴏɴs, Iɴᴄ.
2129 13th Street
Boulder, Colorado 80302
www.shambhala.com

Printed in the United States of America

Shambhala Publications makes every effort to print
on acid-free, recycled paper.

Shambhala Publications is distributed worldwide by
Penguin Random House, Inc., and its subsidiaries.

Designed by Michael Russem

ʟɪʙʀᴀʀʏ ᴏꜰ ᴄᴏɴɢʀᴇss ᴄᴀᴛᴀʟᴏɢɪɴɢ-ɪɴ-ᴘᴜʙʟɪᴄᴀᴛɪᴏɴ ᴅᴀᴛᴀ
Thrangu, Rinpoche, 1933–, author.
Advice from a yogi: an explanation of a Tibetan classic on what is most important /
Khenchen Thrangu; translated by Thrangu Dharmakara Translation
Collaborative. —First edition.
pages   cm
Translated from Tibetan.
ɪsʙɴ 978-1-55939-447-5 (paperback: alk. paper) 1. Dam-pa-sans-rgyas, –1117?
Zal gdams Din-ri bryga rtsa ma. 2. Spiritual life—
Tantric Buddhism. I. Thrangu, Khenchen. II. Title.
BQ8936.D363T57 2015
294.3'420423—dc23
2015000797

CONTENTS

✦ ✦ ✦

TRANSLATORS' INTRODUCTION

✦ ✦ ✦

IN THE SUMMER of 2009, Khenchen Thrangu Rinpoche gave a teaching on *One Hundred Verses of Advice for the People of Dingri* at the Karma Tekchen Zabsal Ling Dharma center in Aurora, Ontario. Among the most inspiring and highly regarded teachings by the Indian tantric master Padampa Sangye, these verses were his final instructions, given as a kind of last testament to his disciples in Dingri, Tibet. Rinpoche brought the text to life in a way that showed how relevant it still is nine hundred years later.

Padampa Sangye lived a very long life—five hundred years, according to Tibetan sources—during which he traveled several times from India to Tibet and China to spread the Dharma. In the first part of his life, he was known as Kamalashila, a student of the great abbot Shantarakshita who was instrumental in bringing Buddhism to Tibet in the eighth century. Invited to Tibet by King Trisong Detsen, Kamalashila participated in one of the most influential debates recorded in Tibetan history—the debate with the Chinese Hashang abbot who argued that one can achieve enlightenment instantaneously without relying on virtuous practices of body and speech. Kamalashila argued to the contrary: for ordinary people, it is necessary to practice the gradual path in order to attain realization and awakening. It was his view of the gradual progression through the stages of the path that held the day and has since formed one of the most important principles adhered to by all schools of Tibetan Buddhism. In addition to his great scholarship, Kamalashila had also mastered the tantric practices and achieved all the different *siddhis*, or accomplishments—the common accomplishments of various clairvoyances, walking very quickly, long life, and so forth, as well as the ultimate accomplishment of enlightenment.

During his time in Tibet, Padampa Sangye was the source for what became known as the Shije or Pacification lineage, so called because it teaches methods for the pacification of suffering. His most famous disciple, the great female yogi Machik Labdrön, was responsible for spreading the chöd practice of offering one's body as a way to perfect generosity and eliminate attachment to oneself. Thus Padampa Sangye is recognized as an important figure in all the lineages of chöd practice that spread in Tibet.

Padampa spent most of his last visit to Tibet in the southern region of Dingri near the border with Nepal. As he prepared to pass away around 1113 CE, the parting advice he gave his disciples was these *One Hundred Verses,* which cover all aspects of Dharma practice, from the beginning of the path to the result. Evidently the householders of twelfth-century Tibet were just as prey to distraction, attachment, and the busyness of worldly life as we are today, and Padampa's final teachings—pithy, forthright, and uncompromising—are as relevant to contemporary practitioners as they were to his audience: Recognize this precious opportunity for spiritual practice. Give up attachment—to your body, your wealth, your family, your home. Develop confidence in karma. Remember the certainty of death as well as the uncertainty of when it will come. Rouse diligence. Look into the nature of your mind. Most important of all, do not postpone Dharma practice. "If you don't have time now," he asks pointedly, "then when will you?"

Though many of Padampa Sangye's verses are easily understood on the first reading, some are more elusive. As always, in his commentary Khenchen Thrangu Rinpoche manages to communicate the essential points in a few simple words. His explanations elaborate the verses that are not immediately clear and unlock a deeper meaning in those that do seem to be clear. Rinpoche also recognizes the particular challenges facing practitioners in contemporary developed societies, and his commentary shows us how we can apply these teachings in our twenty-first-century lives. Though his tone is gentler than Padampa Sangye's, he is no less earnest in urging us forward: "Don't take your time getting around to Dharma practice," he says. "Do it right now."

These teachings were prepared for publication by members of the Thrangu Dharmakara Translation Collaborative. David Karma Choephel translated Thrangu Rinpoche's oral teachings and, along with Tracy Davis and Steve Gilbert, edited them and produced a new translation of Padampa Sangye's verses, in which we attempted to re-create the rhythm of the original Tibetan while reflecting the meaning explained by Rinpoche. If there are any faults, they are solely our own. We would like to express our thanks to Lama Tashi Dondup and the members of KTZL in Aurora, Ontario, who organized the teachings that have become this book; to Alexis Shaw for transcribing the recordings; and to Nikko Odiseos and Michael Wakoff at Shambhala Publications for bringing this book into print. We hope that reading and contemplating these words will help inspire you in your Dharma practice and in your life.

ONE HUNDRED VERSES OF ADVICE

FOR THE PEOPLE OF DINGRI

✦ ✦ ✦

PADAMPA SANGYE

Homage to the guru.

* 1 *

Listen, all you fortunate yogis here in Dingri—
Just as tattered clothes cannot be made like new,
A fatal illness can't be healed by drugs or doctors.
All the people on this earth must surely leave.

* 2 *

Just as rivers all run to the ocean,
Living beings are bound for the same place.

* 3 *

Like a bird that flies off from a treetop,
I cannot stay long; I must move on.

* 4 *

If you waste this life and leave it empty-handed,
You won't easily find a human birth again, people of Dingri.

* 5 *

Strive with body, speech, and mind at Dharma.
It's by far the best thing you can do, people of Dingri.

◆ 6 ◆

Give your heart and mind to the Three Jewels.
Blessings will then naturally arise, people of Dingri.

◆ 7 ◆

Give up this life—focus on the next.
There is not a higher aim than that, people of Dingri.

◆ 8 ◆

Families are as transient as a market throng.
Stop your bickering and nasty talk, people of Dingri.

◆ 9 ◆

Wealth, like an illusion, will beguile you.
Don't be bound in knots of stinginess, people of Dingri.

◆ 10 ◆

Your body's just a sack of filthy stuff.
Don't indulge and pamper it so much, people of Dingri.

◆ 11 ◆

Friends and family are illusory, unreal.
Don't get tangled up in your affections, people of Dingri.

◆ 12 ◆

Your own country's like a nomad's pasture.
Don't be so attached to where you live, people of Dingri.

⁘ 13 ⁘

All beings of the six realms have been your loving parents.
Don't regard them with ideas of "me" and "mine,"
people of Dingri.

⁘ 14 ⁘

Death began approaching from the moment you were born.
There's no time for leisure; rouse yourselves,
people of Dingri.

⁘ 15 ⁘

There's no confusion in the basic state—it's not inherent.
Look into the character of what produces it,
people of Dingri.

⁘ 16 ⁘

Strive without distraction at the Dharma.
It will guide you on the path at death,
people of Dingri.

⁘ 17 ⁘

Cause, result, and karmic ripening are certain.
Turn your back on wrongs and harmful actions,
people of Dingri.

⁘ 18 ⁘

Let all action go, as if a dreamland.
Simply put nonaction into practice, people of Dingri.

✦ 19 ✦

Give up everything that you're attached to.
There is nothing that you need at all, people of Dingri.

✦ 20 ✦

Since you won't stay in this world forever,
Better make your preparations now, people of Dingri.

✦ 21 ✦

When your work is done, there's no time left for Dharma.
Now while it's in mind, make haste to practice,
people of Dingri.

✦ 22 ✦

Though you want the pleasures of a monkey in the forest,
Fires surround the edges of the wood, people of Dingri.

✦ 23 ✦

Birth and aging, sickness, death are rivers
Without bridge or ford; are your boats ready,
people of Dingri?

✦ 24 ✦

Bandits—the five poisons—wait in ambush
At the narrow passes that are birth, death, and the bardo.
Find a lama who will be your escort, people of Dingri.

⬩ 25 ⬩

The unfailing refuge is the teacher.
Always bear the lama on your head, people of Dingri.

⬩ 26 ⬩

Your protection is the lama; rouse devotion
As your fare and you'll get where you want to go,
people of Dingri.

⬩ 27 ⬩

People who have riches end up stingy.
Give to others without any bias, people of Dingri.

⬩ 28 ⬩

People who have power turn to evil.
Humbly place your fingers on your chest, people of Dingri.

⬩ 29 ⬩

In this human world, there are no friends or family.
Place your confidence in Dharma, people of Dingri.

⬩ 30 ⬩

Precious human life is wasted through distraction.
Act decisively right now, people of Dingri.

⋆ 31 ⋆

While you are distracted, death will seize you.
Practice from this very moment on, people of Dingri.

⋆ 32 ⋆

Who knows when the demon Death will come?
Now you need to stand on your own two feet,
people of Dingri.

⋆ 33 ⋆

When you die, there's no one to protect you.
You can only count upon yourselves, people of Dingri.

⋆ 34 ⋆

Like the shadows lengthening at sunset,
Demon Death inexorably comes closer.
Quickly, quickly, run away from him, people of Dingri.

⋆ 35 ⋆

Flowers bloom today and wilt tomorrow.
Don't place any trust in your own body, people of Dingri.

⋆ 36 ⋆

Like the children of the gods while living,
Fearsome as a mob of demons dead—
Your illusory bodies have you tricked, people of Dingri.

· 37 ·

Business done, the market goers scatter.
Friends are sure to leave you in the end, people of Dingri.

· 38 ·

The illusory scarecrows that you build are sure to topple,
So now get ready something that you'll never lose,
people of Dingri.

· 39 ·

Mind is an eagle, sure to fly away.
Now's the time to soar up to the skies, people of Dingri.

· 40 ·

For your kindly parents, beings of the six realms,
Cultivate love, cultivate compassion, people of Dingri.

· 41 ·

Foes are karmic misperceptions of samsara.
Cast off viciousness and hatred, people of Dingri.

· 42 ·

Refuge and reciting mantras purify
Speech's obscurations; give up idle talk, people of Dingri.

· 43 ·

Circumambulation and prostration purify
Bodily obscurations; give up worldly actions,
people of Dingri.

· 44 ·

Fierce devotion purifies your mental habits.
Visualize the lama on your crown, people of Dingri.

· 45 ·

The flesh and bones you're born with all will come apart.
Do not cling to life as if it were eternal, people of Dingri.

· 46 ·

Grasp the finest object, your own constant nature,
Which is free of change and fluctuation, people of Dingri.

· 47 ·

Use the finest jewel, the mind's own nature.
This great wealth will never get depleted, people of Dingri.

· 48 ·

Taste the finest food, samadhi's flavor.
It will soothe the pangs of hunger, people of Dingri.

⬧ 49 ⬧

Sip the best libation, the sweet nectar
Mindfulness, which flows without cessation,
people of Dingri.

⬧ 50 ⬧

Trust the finest friend, awareness wisdom,
Who will never be apart from you, people of Dingri.

⬧ 51 ⬧

Seek the finest child, the babe awareness,
Who is never born and never dies, people of Dingri.

⬧ 52 ⬧

In the empty nature, whirl the lance of pure awareness.
There are no obstructions in the view, people of Dingri.

⬧ 53 ⬧

Train unceasingly in the spontaneous nature.
In conduct, there is nothing to give up or take up,
people of Dingri.

⬧ 54 ⬧

In the thought-free nature, post the sentry nondistraction.
In meditation, there's no torpor or excitement,
people of Dingri.

◆ 55 ◆

The inseparable four kayas are complete within your mind.
Do not fear or hope for the result, people of Dingri.

◆ 56 ◆

The root of both samsara and nirvana
Comes down to mind—and mind has no reality,
people of Dingri.

◆ 57 ◆

Lust and hate arise but leave no trace,
Like birds in flight; don't cling to passing moods,
people of Dingri.

◆ 58 ◆

Unborn dharmakaya, like the essence of the sun,
Is a brilliant radiance that never ebbs or wanes,
people of Dingri.

◆ 59 ◆

Thoughts are like a burglar in an empty house.
There is really nothing there to gain or lose,
people of Dingri.

◆ 60 ◆

Feelings leave no trace, like drawings sketched on water.
Do not cling to these confused appearances,
people of Dingri.

⬩ 61 ⬩

Thoughts of hatred and desire, like rainbows,
Cannot be identified or grasped, people of Dingri.

⬩ 62 ⬩

Mental movements naturally dissolve
Like clouds in the sky; mind has no aim, people of Dingri.

⬩ 63 ⬩

Nonfixation is self-liberated,
Like a breeze, with no clinging to objects, people of Dingri.

⬩ 64 ⬩

Unfixated pure awareness is
Like a rainbow in the sky above.
Experience arises unimpeded, people of Dingri.

⬩ 65 ⬩

Realization of the dharma nature,
Like a mute's dream, is beyond all words, people of Dingri.

⬩ 66 ⬩

Realization, like a young girl's joy,
Is an inexpressible delight, people of Dingri.

✦ 67 ✦

Emptiness and clarity united,
Like the moon's reflection in the water,
Is not blocked or stuck on anything, people of Dingri.

✦ 68 ✦

Like the empty sky above, the mind,
Indivisible emptiness-appearance,
Has no center or periphery, people of Dingri.

✦ 69 ✦

Thought-free nondistraction, like a beauty's mirror,
Has no limits and nothing to prove, people of Dingri.

✦ 70 ✦

Indivisible emptiness-awareness
Is like a reflection in a mirror.
It has no arising and no ceasing, people of Dingri.

✦ 71 ✦

Emptiness inseparable from bliss
Is like the sunlight shining on the snow:
They cannot be differentiated, people of Dingri.

✦ 72 ✦

Deluded speech is traceless, like an echo.
There is nothing to cling to in sound, people of Dingri.

⋄ 73 ⋄

Pain and pleasure's mechanism is
Like a lute's strings and its hollow body.
Your good circumstances come from actions,
people of Dingri.

⋄ 74 ⋄

Samsara and nirvana are self-liberated,
Like a child's game; the mind is free from aims,
people of Dingri.

⋄ 75 ⋄

Outer fabrications are contained within the mind.
Solid ice will melt back into water, people of Dingri.

⋄ 76 ⋄

Ignorance's mechanism works
Like the welling of a meadow spring.
Blocking it won't stop its flowing forth, people of Dingri.

⋄ 77 ⋄

The delusions of samsara and nirvana
Are just like encounters with an enemy.
Practice virtue as your friend and ally, people of Dingri.

· 78 ·

The natural clarity of the five kayas
Is spread before you like a land of gold.
Do not hope or fear, reject or take up, people of Dingri.

· 79 ·

Precious human life's a treasure island.
Don't come back an empty-handed fool, people of Dingri.

· 80 ·

Mahayana Dharma is a wish-fulfilling jewel.
Search long as you may, it will be hard to find again,
people of Dingri.

· 81 ·

Come what may, in this life you'll have clothes and food enough.
Concentrate on what is most important—Dharma practice,
people of Dingri.

· 82 ·

Take on hardships while you are still young.
When you're old, your body won't endure it,
people of Dingri.

· 83 ·

When afflictions come, apply the antidote.
Concepts will be naturally freed, people of Dingri.

⋆ 84 ⋆

Now and then recall samsara's faults.
This will serve to clarify your faith, people of Dingri.

⋆ 85 ⋆

Now be diligent and hold that ground.
This will guide you on the path at death, people of Dingri.

⋆ 86 ⋆

If you don't have time now, then when will you?
You get fed but one time in a hundred, people of Dingri.

⋆ 87 ⋆

Life's uncertain—fleeting as the dew on grass.
Don't be lazy, don't be indolent, people of Dingri.

⋆ 88 ⋆

If you were to slip and fall from here,
Finding human birth again would not be easy,
people of Dingri.

⋆ 89 ⋆

Like the sunlight breaking through the clouds,
The Buddha's teachings are here just for now,
people of Dingri.

⁂ 90 ⁂

You talk cleverly but do not practice.
You're the ones concealing hidden faults, people of Dingri.

⁂ 91 ⁂

Faith is easily swayed by circumstances.
Contemplate the defects of samsara, people of Dingri.

⁂ 92 ⁂

Bad friends naturally lead to bad behavior.
Look to your own mind for making judgments,
people of Dingri.

⁂ 93 ⁂

Ignorant confusion is the demon source of ruin.
Hold fast to awareness and mindfulness, people of Dingri.

⁂ 94 ⁂

Don't cling to the poisons and the path is short.
Generate strong antidotes against them, people of Dingri.

⁂ 95 ⁂

If your diligence is weak, you're lost.
Don the armor so that you will get there, people of Dingri.

⬥ 96 ⬥

Mind's propensities are like old friends
Who keep on coming back; don't chase the past,
people of Dingri.

⬥ 97 ⬥

If your understanding and realization
Are deficient, supplicate your master.
Samadhi will be born within your mind, people of Dingri.

⬥ 98 ⬥

If you wish for future happiness,
Tolerate the hardships of the present.
Buddhahood is right here next to you, people of Dingri.

⬥ 99 ⬥

This old yogi cannot stay in Dingri—
I'm off. Cut through misconceptions now, people of Dingri.

⬥ 100 ⬥

I myself am always undistracted.
Follow my example, people of Dingri.

COMMENTARY

◆ ◆ ◆

KHENCHEN THRANGU

PADAMPA SANGYE was one of the greatest scholars of India. He was also an exceptional meditator, a mahasiddha, who lived for hundreds of years. During his very long life, he lived for many years in India and brought great benefit to many beings there. Then he went to Tibet and to China and benefited many sentient beings there as well. It is through his great kindness that he went to all these places and taught so many beings. That he performed all these deeds and lived for hundreds of years is something that we ordinary sentient beings have trouble understanding; it's something that only the great mahasiddhas can understand. But he came and he taught these *One Hundred Verses of Advice for the People of Dingri,* and to be able to make a Dharma connection through these verses is very fortunate.[1]

At the end of his very long life, Padampa Sangye passed into nirvana in Dingri, and just before he did, he left these instructions as a kind of last testament. At that time, his close disciple Dampa Charchen said to him, "You are about to pass away. When you do, you will go from happiness to happiness, and there will be no difference for you. But all of us who are left behind in Dingri need something to protect us. We need something that we can pray to, something we can have faith and devotion in. Please leave us some testament, some final instructions." In response, Padampa Sangye taught these verses.

⋆ 1 ⋆

Listen, all you fortunate yogis here in Dingri—
Just as tattered clothes cannot be made like new,
A fatal illness can't be healed by drugs or doctors.
All the people on this earth must surely leave.

In the first few verses, Padampa Sangye explains why he is leaving this testament and why the practitioners of Dingri need to listen to these instructions. He gives the reason through a series of analogies: When your clothes get tattered, you can't make them into new clothes again. And when you have a fatal illness and you are about to die, seeing the doctor won't help. You have to go. We all have to go. Everything is impermanent; death is approaching for everyone.

• 2 •

Just as rivers all run to the ocean,
Living beings are bound for the same place.

Rivers may be long or short, they may be broad or narrow, but they all go to the same place: their waters all flow toward the ocean. Similarly, some people have long lives, some have short lives, but all of us are headed for the same final destination of death. There is no way anyone can avoid it. Padampa Sangye is saying, "All you fortunate students are impermanent. And because you are impermanent and are going to die, you need to listen to these instructions well."

Padampa Sangye taught these final instructions at the time he passed away, and the reason he passed away was to demonstrate impermanence. Padampa Sangye had already lived for hundreds of years, and in fact he probably could have lived for hundreds of years more, but many of his students, because of their ego-clinging, were starting to get attached to the idea of permanence, and he passed away in order to dispel that. This is why, in these instructions of his last testament, the main subject is impermanence.

• 3 •

Like a bird that flies off from a treetop,
I cannot stay long; I must move on.

All sentient beings, whoever they are, have to move on. Everyone in this world—big, important people and small, unimportant people;

those who have a lot of wealth and power and those who have none—
must pass on. All humans have to pass on, and all animals, too, from
big, strong animals to tiny insects—gradually their lives will come to
an end, and they must all pass along. It's like a bird in a treetop. Does
the bird stay there for long? No, it flies right off. In the same way, we
all have to go. Padampa Sangye is saying that it's time for him to go
on to the next place, and this is why he is giving these instructions
that are in accord with the Dharma. He is saying, "You need to listen to these instructions because there is one place where we are all
headed. I am about to go there, and eventually all of you will, too.
When we go, we want to make sure it turns out well; we don't want
it to go badly. If you want it to go well, you need to listen to these
instructions."

* 4 *

It is wonderful to have the motivation to enter the gate of the Dharma
and to study and practice. This is an unmistaken motivation. But even
if the initial motivation that brings you to the Dharma is very good,
the contemporaneous motivation—the motivation of an ordinary individual at the actual time of study or practice—might not be so good.
You might come under the power of the afflictions, or you might have
a neutral motivation.

When practicing and studying, it's important to have a motivation
that is free from affliction. Among the various pure motivations, the
most important is the wish to help ourselves and others, the vast motivation of the Mahayana, which means acting for the sake of all our former mothers, all sentient beings, who are as limitless as space. You may
already have faith, respect, and excitement about the Dharma, and the
pure motivation of bodhichitta. Still, it is good to recall and reinforce
that motivation from time to time. It helps your mind to go toward
the Dharma, the Dharma to become the path, and the path to dispel
confusion.[2]

We need to be extremely careful in this life. We need to practice the Dharma; we need to use our life for the Dharma. As Padampa Sangye says:

> If you waste this life and leave it empty-handed,
> You won't easily find a human birth again, people of Dingri.

We don't want to leave this life empty-handed. What does "empty-handed" mean? Well, when we are born, do we come into the world fully clothed, with all the knowledge, wealth, and possessions we need? We don't. We come into this world as newborn babes naked, with nothing, and we have to acquire it all.

Over the course of this human life, we do various things, and if we come to the end of our lives and think, "Oh, no! I didn't do anything to prepare for the next life," that's when we find ourselves empty-handed. All the things we've done for the purpose of this life won't help us at the moment of death. In order to make sure that we don't leave this life with empty hands, we need to accomplish the Dharma properly. If we can have some signs of practice, if we can say to ourselves at the time of death, "I practiced well and I achieved this result," that is first-rate. But even if we can't do that, at the very least we need to be able to say, "I entered the gate of the Dharma and did some Dharma practice." If at least we can say that, we won't be leaving this life empty-handed.

Whatever little bit of practice we do is helpful. If when we are young, we recite one million OM MANI PADME HŪM mantras, then at the time of death, at least we can say to ourselves, "I did a million MANI mantras and that is really good." Or maybe we can say, "I did the four special preliminary practices one hundred thousand times each and that is really good." On the other hand, if we end our life without having done anything at all, that is leaving empty-handed.

Now we have this human body, and with it we can do something meaningful. But if we don't accomplish anything with this life, we will come to the end of it and have nothing. This is why we need to make sure that we do our Dharma practice now, while we are full of life, healthy, and able to practice, so that we do not leave this life empty-handed.

The second line of this verse reads, "You won't easily find a human birth again, people of Dingri." We have a human life now; when we die and take rebirth, will we be able to gain a human life again? If we do not leave this life empty-handed—that is, if we listen to these instructions, keep them in mind, and actually put them into practice—then we can attain a human life again.

Attaining a human life is not said to be impossible, but it is difficult for those who waste this life. This is why we need to keep these instructions in mind and tell ourselves, "I am not going to leave this life empty-handed." It is important not to waste this life but to practice the Dharma.

To attain a human life is extremely fortunate, and since we have this good fortune, we need to use it. We came into this world empty-handed. To leave empty-handed would be senseless: we wouldn't be able to attain a human life in the future. But if we act in accord with the Dharma by following these instructions, keeping them in mind, and putting them into practice, then we can attain a human life without difficulty.

◦ 5 ◦

What do we need to do in order to make sure that we do not leave this life empty-handed? The next verse reads:

Strive with body, speech, and mind at Dharma.
It's by far the best thing you can do, people of Dingri.

Striving at the Dharma means being diligent about the Dharma. How do we do that? We need to do it with our body, speech, and mind—all three. Is it enough to be diligent with just our body or just our speech or just our mind? No, it's not enough.

For example, I am a monk. I wear Dharma robes and I've shaved my head, so people think I must be a real Dharma practitioner. But this alone is not enough. We have to ask ourselves: Are the words I say good, helpful words, or are they not really in accord with the Dharma? Do I spend my time lying, saying harsh things, and talking behind people's backs? Or do I actually use my speech well? If we are all right in terms of what we do with our body, we also have to make sure that we are all right in what we do in our speech.

But if our body is all right and our speech is all right, then can we do whatever we want with our mind? No, we need to make sure that with our mind too we are truly compatible with the Dharma. We need to have a kind heart, love, compassion, faith and devotion, and all the other positive qualities. Otherwise, if our mind is filled with greed, aversion, delusion, pride, malice, and all sorts of unvirtuous thoughts, then no matter how virtuous we are with our body and speech, it won't be all that helpful.

We need to be very careful with our mind as well as our body and our speech. For example, I could take out my mala and start reciting OM MAṆI PADME HŪṂ, but what kinds of thoughts are in my mind? We have to look at our mind and see: Do I have love and compassion in my mind? Do I have faith and devotion in my mind? Otherwise, if I'm reciting OM MAṆI PADME HŪṂ but my mind is filled with afflictions and negative emotions, that is not Dharma at all. We need to make sure our body, our speech, and our mind are all being applied to the Dharma. We need to be as diligent about Dharma practice as we can, and that means working with our body, speech, and mind together. As Padampa Sangye says, this is by far the best thing we can do.

Ideally, whatever we do should be something that helps ourselves and others. If that isn't possible, then at least what we are doing should help ourselves. Otherwise, if we don't help ourselves or help others, then our lives end up being meaningless. For that reason, we need to strive diligently with body, speech, and mind at the Dharma.

⋅ 6 ⋅

Give your heart and mind to the Three Jewels.
Blessings will then naturally arise, people of Dingri.

The next verse of advice addresses our motivation, and here the text uses an analogy. The Tibetan literally reads, "Give your lungs, your heart, and your chest." But this doesn't mean that you have to rip out your heart and lungs and give them to the Three Jewels. What it means is that you need to have faith and belief.

You have to give your heart and mind to the Three Jewels, and you do this with the three kinds of faith: sincere faith, the faith of wishing, and the faith of belief. Sincere faith is thinking, "The Dharma is wonderful and I need to practice it." Wishing faith is thinking, "If I practice the Dharma, then in the future I can gain a wonderful result. I can become a buddha." The faith of belief is to believe exactly that. With these three types of faith, we direct our mind to the Three Jewels.

How do we give our heart and mind to the Three Jewels? We go for refuge to the Three Jewels as the teacher, the path, and our companions on the path. First, we go for refuge to the Buddha as the teacher. How is it that the Buddha teaches us? As it is said in the oral instructions:

> He can't remove beings' suffering with his hands,
> Nor can he transfer his realization to others.
> He liberates by teaching the peace of the dharmata.

It is not as though the Buddha sees all these wandering sentient beings and if we say to him, "Oh, Buddha, I'm suffering. I've got an illness. Please take it away," he can reach out his hand and pluck it away from us. That is not how the Buddha takes away our suffering. It is not as if the Buddha can simply bestow upon us all the knowledge and the qualities we lack. We go for refuge to the Buddha as our teacher, and he teaches us the Dharma. He gives us the instructions: "If you give up doing wrongs and misdeeds, if you practice virtue, this will bring you happiness." When we practice these instructions and keep them in mind, they can help us. It is by receiving the instructions, keeping them in mind, and putting them into practice that we go for refuge to the Buddha as our teacher.

Then we go for refuge to the Dharma as the path. Can the Dharma immediately protect us from suffering? It cannot. We first have to take it as the path. As we put it into practice, it is a method for freeing us from samsara's suffering and from the afflictions. In this way we go for refuge to the Dharma as the path.

Then we go for refuge to the sangha as our companions on the path. The sangha of practitioners—whether ordained or not—are our companions who have faith in the Dharma, and they can advise us. They help us develop belief in the Dharma when we do not have it. They help us develop faith and devotion. They help us generate renunciation and weariness with samsara. They help us increase our love and compassion. The people who help us in this way are our companions, the sangha. When we take refuge in the sangha and develop these qualities, it is a sign of having gone for refuge in the Dharma.

When we go for refuge to the Buddha as the teacher, to the Dharma as the path, thinking, "I need to practice this Dharma," and to the sangha as our companions on the path, then, as the text says, "Blessings will then naturally arise." The blessings will come automatically. In this way, we need to give our heart and mind to the Three Jewels. If we do this, we will definitely receive blessings.

* 7 *

Give up this life—focus on the next.
There is not a higher aim than that, people of Dingri.

The subject of this verse is impermanence. Death and impermanence are not very pleasant topics. We find it rather uncomfortable, even depressing, to think about death and impermanence, but in fact it is extremely helpful, because thinking about impermanence encourages us. If we contemplate impermanence, we can accomplish something of meaning and purpose.

As the great yogi Milarepa said:

> First I went to the mountains from the fear of death,
> But now I've seized the stronghold of deathlessness.

Out of fear of death and impermanence, Milarepa went to the mountains; then he meditated there, and the result was that he no longer needed to fear death. This is how meditation on impermanence helped him.

Likewise, in one sutra it says, "The best of all meditations is the meditation on impermanence." The reason is that in the beginning, it is the condition that leads us to practice the Dharma. In the middle, it is the rod that spurs us on to practice, and in the end, it is the companion to attaining the result.

First, meditating on impermanence is the condition that leads us to practice the Dharma. Generally, we are involved with both Dharma practice and worldly affairs. Normally, if we have to choose between these two, we choose worldly activity. We get distracted by all kinds of worldly affairs and are not able to really engage in Dharma practice. But if we meditate on impermanence and truly see how we are impermanent, we'll develop world-weariness and renunciation that will lead us to think, "I really have to practice Dharma." Meditating on impermanence is the condition that encourages us to practice the Dharma.

Once I met someone, and when I told him that I was a Buddhist, he said, "Buddhists are no good. Religion is something that should inspire people and give them strength, but Buddhists only talk about impermanence, emptiness, selflessness, and suffering. You always talk about negative things and never give people any encouragement." Maybe he's right. We do always talk about impermanence and suffering and selflessness, but there's a good reason: it encourages us to practice the Dharma.

The second reason for meditating on impermanence is that it is the rod that spurs us to diligence. Sometimes we lose our diligence and get a bit lazy; we don't feel the wish to practice Dharma. At that point, if we think about suffering and contemplate impermanence, it will spur us to practice. If we lack diligence or faith, we can gain diligence and faith.

People often ask, "I really like the Dharma; I really want to practice Dharma, but I just can't seem to do it. What should I do?" The answer is to meditate on the four thoughts that turn the mind to the Dharma and in particular to meditate on death and impermanence, because this is the rod that spurs us to diligence.

Finally, meditating on impermanence is the companion to obtaining the result. First it encourages us to enter the gate of the Dharma, then it encourages us to be diligent, and through our diligence the good results of the Dharma come right into our hands. How do we meditate on impermanence? As Padampa Sangye says, give up this life and focus on the next. When you have a choice between Dharma activities and the affairs of this world, you should forget about the worldly concerns. Put them aside. Concentrate on Dharma practice instead. Give up this life.

If you think the affairs of this life are more important, you will put most of your effort into them and end up setting Dharma activity aside. You'll concentrate so much on this life that you cannot put the Dharma into practice at all. You'll forget the Dharma entirely.

How does it help you to give up this life and focus on the next? It helps because it brings you the highest aim. In other words, you come to attain a result. Then you can say to yourself, "I did something that was really meaningful. I truly accomplished something with this life."

◆ 8 ◆

Families are as transient as a market throng.
Stop your bickering and nasty talk, people of Dingri.

In families there is a particular danger of getting angry with one another, quarreling, or saying nasty things to one another. It's important to give up nastiness and bickering with those who are close to you. There's not as great a danger of this happening with people who are distant; when you bicker and say mean things, it's generally with the people who are close to you. This instruction is primarily for householders.

Why should we give up bickering and nasty talk? Although we might think that our family will stay together for a long time, actually families are not that stable. They are impermanent. It's like the crowd that gathers at a market or at a conference: people come together at a conference for a few days or maybe a week, and then it's over and everyone goes home. It's the same with our families. Although we might think that our families will last a long time, they will not last forever, and so it is important to give up saying harsh things to one another, to give up bickering and nasty talk.

People often ask me, "What is the best way to make sure our children grow up to appreciate the Dharma and become Buddhists?" The advice I give is to get along in your family. If the members of a family all get along and are kind and loving, honest and straightforward, peaceful and affectionate with one another, the children will see it and say, "You know, Dharma practitioners must be all right." They consequently develop an interest in the Dharma and eventually start to practice. This is why it is very important not to bicker or quarrel or fight.

· 9 ·

Practicing the Dharma is important, but not simply because someone says to us, "You must practice the Dharma." We have to know the underlying purpose. When we genuinely understand the reasons, we can enter the gate of the Dharma.

What prevents us from practicing the Dharma? Attachment to our wealth, body, friends and relatives, country, and so forth. Being attached to and fixated on these often makes us unable to engage in Dharma practice. For this, Padampa Sangye gives some advice—first, not to be attached to property and wealth:

> Wealth, like an illusion, will beguile you.
> Don't be bound in knots of stinginess, people of Dingri.

In general, wealth and possessions possess appearances so bright and dazzling that we think, "Oh, I can't live without that; I absolutely must have it." We think it is so important, and we get beguiled and fooled by it. External appearances deceive us. Actually, sometimes we need wealth and possessions, but we should use them to benefit ourselves or others or both. Doing this fits well with the Dharma. But if we are so bound by knots of stinginess that we aren't able to use our wealth to help either ourselves or others, it doesn't do anyone any good.

As the great master Sakya Pandita said, "If you find yourself unable either to use your wealth or to give it away but imagine yourself to be rich, it would be far easier just to imagine that you have a mountain made of gold." You should use your wealth and possessions to help yourself and others. If instead you refuse either to spend your money on yourself or to give it away and you just hoard it out of stinginess, what good does that do you? It would be far easier just to imagine that some great mountain is made of gold and pretend that you own it. To have a lot of wealth but not use it is actually very difficult for you. It's far easier just to pretend that you own a huge mountain of gold. "Don't be bound in knots of stinginess" is advice to use our wealth and possessions to benefit both ourselves and others.

* 10 *

Your body's just a sack of filthy stuff.
Don't indulge and pamper it so much, people of Dingri.

We also need to give up attachment to our body. There is no benefit in cherishing our body and considering it overly important. Of course, we do need to attend to our hygiene and health. But if we are overly attached and think, "I can't do Dharma practice, I might get exhausted; I might get sick," this doesn't help us at all.

If we look at the body, we see that there actually is nothing about it that is very meaningful or very pleasant. As Padampa Sangye says, the body is just a sack of filthy stuff. We might want to make it look nice, to indulge and pamper it, but there isn't much use in doing that. Padampa Sangye says, "Don't indulge and pamper it so much, people of Dingri." Don't cherish your body.

Generally, it is as the great master Shantideva taught: Now that we have this body, we need to use it as a slave to practice the Dharma to benefit ourselves and others. We have this body and we need to put it to good use, which means putting it to work to serve the Dharma. If we employ our body to serve the Dharma, we can benefit ourselves and others. In that sense, this body is good. When we speak of the precious human body, the human body that is like a wish-fulfilling jewel, this is what we mean. When we call it the jewel-like human body, does this mean that the body itself is like a jewel? No. The body is nothing but a sack of filth filled with blood and guts and gore. But if we use our body to help ourselves and to help others, it has the potential to achieve a great result. In this sense, it is a precious, jewel-like body. But if we pamper it, thinking, "Oh, no, I can't do that—my body is precious and I might get sick," that doesn't help us in any way. Don't indulge and pamper your body, and be diligent about Dharma practice.

✦ 11 ✦

> *Friends and family are illusory, unreal.*
> *Don't get tangled up in your affections, people of Dingri.*

We need to give up attachment to our friends and relatives and make sure that they don't become a condition that prevents us from practicing the Dharma. Friends and relatives are illusory—they have no real essence and are not really all that stable. They don't last long. This is because the human body itself doesn't last very long—forty, fifty, sixty, seventy years, maybe eighty years at best. One day we'll have to move on. One day our friends and relatives will have to move on. It's all illusory and unreal.

You should not let yourself get tangled up in your affections. You might think, "I really need to practice the Dharma, but there are all my friends and relatives—I need to help them. Still, I do need to practice the Dharma. What am I going to do?" So you might say to yourself, "Okay, I'm going to practice Dharma for one day," but when that day comes, you say, "Oh, I can't practice all day long today because there are other things I have to finish doing. Well, then, I'll just practice Dharma for one hour. But if I practice for one hour, I won't be able to finish this or that." So you never get around to your Dharma practice. You should not have this sort of attachment; you should not tie yourself down out of fondness. You need to be diligent about the Dharma—that is what will help you. Understanding this is the method for giving up attachment to friends and relatives.

* 12 *

Attachment to our country and our region can also prevent us from practicing the Dharma, so we need to give it up. As it says:

> Your own country's like a nomad's pasture.
> Don't be so attached to where you live, people of Dingri.

Sometimes we become very attached to our home—our house, our region, our country—and we think, "It's so wonderful here; I can't give up this place. I should practice Dharma a little bit, but I can't really do that here. This house is no good for practice; I don't have everything I need; it's a problem." This sort of attachment becomes an obstacle that prevents us from practicing the Dharma. Such attachment doesn't help us in any way.

Our own country is said to be like a nomad's pasture. A nomad goes to one pasture for a little while and then moves on to the next pasture, and then to the next and the next. Similarly, we also move from place to place. We might stay in one place for a year or two, but then we'll probably move along. Our lives are always changing. Life is impermanent by nature, and we are always moving on to another place. Having attachment to a place is not helpful. What is far better is to practice the Dharma. Don't be so attached to where you live.

Attachment to wealth and possessions, to our body, to our friends and relatives, and to our country can become an obstacle that prevents us from practicing the Dharma. We should give up such attachment.

◆ 13 ◆

When we feel either aversion or attachment, generally it is toward the beings of the six realms of samsara.

> *All beings of the six realms have been your loving parents.*
> *Don't regard them with ideas of "me" and "mine," people of Dingri.*

We think, "I'm me, and this is mine. That is other; that is someone else's." When we start thinking about the difference between ourselves and others, we begin to cherish ourselves and we feel aversion and jealousy toward others. This is not how we want to be.

We need to have an equal feeling toward all. All the beings in the six realms have been our parents in past lives, and we should view them all equally. Otherwise, if we think, "This is mine and that is another's; these are my friends and those are my enemies," and set up this distinction between the two, it increases our attachment and aversion. We need to eliminate such attachment and aversion.

◆ 14 ◆

We need to be diligent. We may think we can stretch out, relax, and have a good time, but we need to give up this kind of thinking. As it says:

> *Death began approaching from the moment you were born.*
> *There's no time for leisure; rouse yourselves, people of Dingri.*

The moment we say, "I've been born," someone can reply, "Yes, and you are going to die. The sign of your death approaching has already appeared." We may think we can put our feet up, relax for a while, and take it easy, but that's not how it is. Instead we need to realize, "I need to practice the instructions that will help me at the time of death. I don't have much time; I need to be diligent about this." We absolutely need to rouse our diligence. As described earlier, the meditation on impermanence is the rod that spurs us to diligence.

◆ 15 ◆

There's no confusion in the basic state—it's not inherent.
Look into the character of what produces it, people of Dingri.

If we practice the Dharma, can we achieve a result? We can, and the reason is that the confusion of our samsaric world does not exist in the basic state. The confused samsaric appearances of the world are like dreams; they arise ephemerally. Other than an empty nature, there is really nothing that produces them, so look into the character of what produces them. If we do so, we will be able to achieve the ultimate result. Confused samsaric appearances can disappear. We can eliminate suffering and afflictions. Afflictions are not inherent; they do not primordially exist, so we can eliminate them.

◆ 16 ◆

Strive without distraction at the Dharma.
It will guide you on the path at death, people of Dingri.

We need to apply ourselves diligently now to practice the Dharma without distraction. The benefit is that when we come to the point of our death, we will have a good path that we can go along without any difficulty.

Often we think that we have so many things to do in this world. We want to practice the Dharma, but somehow we just don't have the time. In fact, we do have an opportunity to practice the Dharma without distraction, and this is due to the kindness of Jesus Christ—thanks to the spread of Christianity all over the world, Sunday is a day off! This provides a great opportunity to practice the Dharma: every month there are four days when we can practice without distraction. Not only that, in most developed countries people also have Saturdays off, so there are eight days a month when we can practice the Dharma without distraction. In addition, many people leave work a little early on Friday afternoons, so if we have diligence, this is another opportunity to practice the Dharma without distraction. This is all very beneficial. Getting lost in distraction instead—going to the beach to get a suntan and enjoy ourselves—won't help us at all. It will only create an obstacle to our Dharma practice. If we exert ourselves in Dharma practice, then when we come to the difficulty facing us at death, we will have done something helpful.

* 17 *

Cause, result, and karmic ripening are certain.
Turn your back on wrongs and harmful actions, people of Dingri.

It is important to think carefully about karma, cause, and effect. Of the actions that we perform with our body, speech, and mind, the positive, beneficial actions will lead to a positive ripening and a good result. Likewise, harmful actions will definitely lead to a bad result. This is certain and true. That is why we need to avoid all wrongs and harmful actions, because they will definitely ripen upon us. In terms of the ripening of karma, according to Buddhist teachings, there are four types: karma that is visibly experienced, karma that is experienced on rebirth, karma that is experienced in other lifetimes, and karma that is not definitely experienced.

Karma that is visibly experienced comes from a very strong, powerful action done with a strong motivation. Because of the strength of the
action, the result ripens in this very life. Some actions are not quite as
strong, so they don't ripen in this lifetime, but they are strong enough that
they will definitely ripen in our next lifetime. This is karma that is experienced upon rebirth. And some actions are not nearly as strong, so they
won't ripen either in this lifetime or in our next lifetime, but they will definitely be experienced at some time in the future, when all the right conditions come together. This is karma that is experienced in other lifetimes.

These three are types of karma that we will definitely experience, but
there is also karma that is not definitely experienced. This is a very weak
karma, a small action. If it is a misdeed or an unvirtuous karma, then if
we confess it, it will disappear. If it is a virtuous action, then if we regret
it, it will disappear. This is the fourth type, karma that is not definitely
experienced.

These are the four ways that karma can ripen upon us, the ways cause
and effect works. An action that is a cause will definitely bring a result. If
our actions are wrongs or harmful actions—if we commit misdeeds and
unvirtuous acts—the results will definitely ripen upon us. This is why
we need to turn our backs on wrongs and harmful actions.

⁕ 18 ⁕

We need to be diligent about our practice, but we also need to do our
work. Sometimes it feels as if we have a lot of things to do and this con-
flicts with practicing the Dharma. When these two are in conflict, the
one that we should consider more important is practicing the Dharma.
As it says:

> Let all action go, as if a dreamland.
> Simply put nonaction into practice, people of Dingri.

When we work, we often put a lot of effort into it, but we have to realize
that actually it's just like a dream. All the work that we've done is in the

past. It doesn't help us anymore. It has already happened, so it is like a dreamland. Simply put nonaction into practice. Nonaction here means Dharma. Simply put the Dharma into practice.

✦ 19 ✦

We need to give up all attachment to everything. As described before, this could be attachment to our body, wealth and possessions, friends and relatives, or home. Attachment to these creates obstacles to our practicing the Dharma, and we end up doing a lot of pointless things. As it says:

> *Give up everything that you're attached to.*
> *There is nothing that you need at all, people of Dingri.*

If we are attached to something, this doesn't help us in any way. It is far better for us to practice the Dharma.

✦ 20 ✦

> *Since you won't stay in this world forever,*
> *Better make your preparations now, people of Dingri.*

In the future, we are all going to die. All humans have to pass away at some point. We live in this world for only a few years. We can't stay for hundreds or thousands of years. We have to move on.

Where do we go when we die? In the Buddhist view, we go from this life to the next life. After we die, the appearances of the bardo, the between state, arise, and from the bardo we take birth in the next life. That might be a good rebirth or it might be a bad rebirth. The cause of a good rebirth is practicing virtue in this life. The cause of a bad rebirth is misdeeds, nonvirtue, and the afflictions. In order to make sure we take a good rebirth, we had better make our preparations.

The Dharma recently started spreading in the West, and many people have a lot of faith and belief in it. They believe in karma, cause, and effect; they believe that there are future lives and that this is meaningful and important. These people need to strive to practice virtue and to give up nonvirtue as much as possible. It is important to accomplish the Dharma as preparation for the next life.

There are also people in the West who are not entirely certain about future lives. They think, "I'm not sure. We can't see this. Maybe it's possible, but maybe there are no future lives." We can't say with 100 percent certainty that there are future lives, but we also cannot definitely say that there are not. But whether there are future lives or not, it is still a good idea to prepare for them now.

If we make preparations for the next life now, then when the time of our death arrives, if there is a future life, our preparations will stand us in good stead. And if we prepare for the next life but it turns out that there is no future life, it doesn't really matter. There is no harm at all in having made the preparations.

On the other hand, if we don't prepare for the next life but at the time of death it turns out that there is a future life, then it's too late to do anything, and that is a difficult situation. That is why it is important now to practice virtue and to give up misdeeds and nonvirtue. We need to be diligent and practice the Dharma as much as possible.

⁘ 21 ⁘

When your work is done, there's no time left for Dharma.
Now while it's in mind, make haste to practice, people of Dingri.

We need to make our preparations now, and we need to be diligent about it. We may think, "I really want to practice the Dharma, but right now I'm really busy, and I have a lot of things to do. I'll get to the Dharma when my work is done." This way of thinking is an obstacle that will prevent us from practicing the Dharma. If we are busy doing something right now, then when we are done, something else will come up that will keep us busy, and when that's done, there will be something else, and something else after that. It's just one thing after another that we have to do. We end up with no opportunity to practice the Dharma at all.

Padampa Sangye says, "Now while it's in mind, make haste to practice." When we think, "I've got to practice the Dharma," we need to go and practice diligently right away. Otherwise, all kinds of things will come up that we think we need to do first, and we'll never get around to practicing.

It is said that we should be as diligent in our Dharma practice as we would be if our hair were on fire. If our hair caught fire, we would immediately do whatever we could to put out the flames. We need to practice the Dharma with this kind of diligence.

Another analogy from old instruction texts is the blind man who is lost in the middle of a huge, flat plain. He can't see anything, and he has no idea where he is or where he's going. He doesn't know which way is east or west or south or north. He has no idea how to get back home. As he wanders around, wondering, "Where do I go and how can I get home?" he hears the sound of a cow munching on the grass. When he hears this, he thinks, "Ah, this cow probably has an owner, so if I grab on to her tail, she'll lead me to where I need to go." By listening to the sounds, he finds the cow, grabs on to her tail, and hangs on. The cow wanders around eating its supper, having all the grass it wants, and finally comes back to its barn, and there's a person there, so the blind man can say, "I'm lost. How do I get home?" In the same way, now that we have this chance to practice the Dharma, we have to grab on to it right away. We have to hold on and not let go.

Sometimes we need to encourage ourselves to be diligent about practice, even if we have a high level of practice. To develop the necessary faith and devotion in the Dharma, the preliminaries are most helpful. It is often said that the preliminaries are more profound than the actual practice. Of course, the actual practice is very profound, but we are all ordinary individuals and therefore we sometimes fall prey to laziness and sloth. To address this, we should do the preliminary meditations.

Meditate upon impermanence. Meditate upon renunciation and world-weariness. This is very beneficial and also easy, because we can actually see that things are impermanent. As Lord Milarepa said:

> I take all that appears and exists as a text;
> I've never studied texts in ink.

To meditate upon impermanence, we can just look at our country, our home, our friends and family, and all the places we've been. It's easy to see that they are changing and impermanent. It's the same with karma and with our precious human body. If we look at these appearances, we can see the nature of how they actually are. This will help us develop belief in the Dharma and inspire us to practice.

◆ 22 ◆

In order to attain buddhahood, we need to be diligent about the Dharma, particularly practice and study, at which time we should rouse a pure motivation.

> *Though you want the pleasures of a monkey in the forest,*
> *Fires surround the edges of the wood, people of Dingri.*

Earlier, in the context of the preliminary training of the mind, we saw how meditation on impermanence encourages us to practice the Dharma. This topic continues in the next verse with an analogy of the pleasures of monkeys in the forest. The monkeys may be eating fruit, playing, and enjoying themselves. But it doesn't turn out well in the end, because the forest is surrounded by fire and there's no escape. The meaning of this analogy is not immediately obvious. The forest represents this world. Here we are having a grand time just like those monkeys, making plans for the future and getting distracted by worldly affairs. This brings feelings of happiness or unhappiness that overcome

us, so that we do not remember the Dharma. The fire around the edges
of this forest represents death waiting for us. Aging, sickness, and death
are inevitable. As the masters of the Kadampa school said, "The end of
meeting is parting; the end of birth is dying." There is no way out for
us. We are in great danger. Actually, there is one way to escape: If we
practice the Dharma, we will not be overwhelmed by suffering. We will
not lose ourselves to pain or happiness. We will be able to free ourselves
from difficulties and eventually come to the ultimate result; things will
get better and better for us. Since getting distracted from the Dharma
will make our situation more difficult, we need to understand our circumstances well.

· 23 ·

Birth and aging, sickness, death are rivers
Without bridge or ford; are your boats ready, people of Dingri?

The previous verse was about the danger we are facing, and this one
tells us how to approach it. In this analogy, we come to great rivers that
represent birth, aging, sickness, and death. We need to cross these rivers, but there is neither a bridge nor a shallow place where we can cross
easily. What do we need? If we have a good boat, we can easily cross the
rivers, but without a boat it will be difficult and even dangerous. And if
we know that there are rivers ahead that have no bridges or shallows, we
can prepare a boat for the crossing.

The river of birth refers to your next rebirth. When you die and
migrate to the next realm, you need to make sure to take a good birth.
The boat that can take you across this river is known as the bardo
instructions on blocking or choosing a rebirth. According to these
instructions, if you see yourself about to take a bad rebirth during the
bardo period between death and rebirth, you can realize what is happening and prevent a bad rebirth by visualizing the Three Jewels, generating faith and devotion, and supplicating them to be reborn in a good

body. This is how you can use your own intelligence to choose a good rebirth. In the best of circumstances, you may be reborn in a pure realm or at least in a good human body where you encounter the Dharma. If you understand these instructions, you can train in them in preparation for crossing the river of birth.

The rivers of aging, sickness, and death can be traversed through the power of meditation. There are the instructions on taking death, taking the bardo, and taking pain and sickness as the path. We can use all of them so that we do not become overwhelmed and do not experience much suffering. There are many different instructions that we can study and practice so that such circumstances turn out well.

Another way to free ourselves from the sufferings of birth, aging, sickness, and death is to do the practice of the Medicine Buddha. If we meditate upon, supplicate, and recite the mantra of the Medicine Buddha, it is certain that he will come and help us because the Medicine Buddha made twelve great aspirations to save all beings from suffering. This is a very good practice to do.

Those who experience a lot of fear can supplicate Green Tara because she made a strong commitment to save people from the eight or sixteen types of fear.[3] Visualize Green Tara in front of you, supplicate her, and do the common Green Tara practice. This is very helpful. Whether you recite the twenty-one praises of Tara or her essence mantra, OM TĀRE TUTTĀRE TURE SVĀHĀ, think that Lady Tara is present in front of you. If you are able to visualize clearly, visualize all twenty-one Taras in front of you. If you are not able to do that, visualize just Green Tara. Think that she is present in front of you.

Some people have doubt and think that if they don't see her, she's not really there. They wonder, "If I'm just imagining this, how can it help me?" In actuality, our physical eyes see only the appearances of this world, so we can't see Green Tara with our physical eyes. But Green Tara has the eyes of wisdom, with which she can see us just as we are. Because she can see us, if we pray or supplicate or make aspirations to her, we will be able to accomplish our purposes. Therefore we think that Tara is truly present in front of us.

Reciting the twenty-one praises or the OM TĀRE TUTTĀRE TURE SVĀHĀ mantra while thinking that she is present in front of us as we visualize and supplicate her is the first of four visualizations. In the second visualization, Green Tara is present in front, with her right hand in the posture of supreme generosity and her left hand in the mudra of protecting from fear. We think that she reaches out and places her hand on top of our head and that as she does so, we are freed from all fears, suffering, and other problems. They cannot harm us, and we no longer need to be afraid of them.

The third visualization is to supplicate Tara, who then sees us with her wisdom eyes. Because of her great wisdom and compassion, nectar flows from her body into the crown of our head.

In the fourth visualization, with either the twenty-one Taras or just Green Tara in front, the visualization melts into light and then dissolves into us. We think that our own body is transformed into the body of Green Tara. It appears, yet its essence is empty. We recite the essence mantra, and through doing this, in the short term we are able to free ourselves from all fears and suffering. Ultimately we can free ourselves from suffering and all the terrors of the lower realms.

If we do these practices, we are prepared; we have a boat to carry us across the rivers of suffering. We need to put effort into the methods that can free us from birth, aging, sickness, and death. Among these methods, those that can help us through birth, death, and the bardo are of particular importance and are the subject of the next verse.

· 24 ·

Bandits—the five poisons—wait in ambush
At the narrow passes that are birth, death, and the bardo.
Find a lama who will be your escort, people of Dingri.

Birth, death, and the bardo are like a narrow passage such as a steep-walled ravine with just a very small path. As we walk down this path, bandits, robbers—the five poisons—are waiting in ambush for us. Who can help us through this dangerous situation? Find a lama who will be your escort, Padampa Sangye says. We need a teacher to guide us.

The five poisons wait for us in the bardo. The bardo between death and rebirth is actually a series of different bardos. One is the bardo of dying. During the process of dying, we often experience a lot of attachment to the things of this life. Due to these attachments, we may feel hatred or anger toward others. We may feel intense fear of our impending death. If we are overcome by these afflictions and fear, not only do we experience temporary suffering, but passing through the bardo becomes difficult.

We want to make sure that we do not take a bad rebirth; we want a good rebirth. Ideally, we want to be reborn in a pure realm. If not, at least we want to be reborn in a human body in which we can practice the Dharma. This is very important. What can get in the way of that? The afflictions are waiting in ambush for us. At the time of death, they arise, and we will feel attachment, aversion, hatred, jealousy, fear, and other emotions. We may also experience suffering at that time because we lack good methods for taking death as the path. We must make sure that this doesn't happen. The instructions on the bardo say that we must not be overcome by afflictions or fear. In order to take the path to a good rebirth, we need to remember the Buddha, the Dharma, the sangha, and our yidam deities. Through remembering them and supplicating and praying to them, our mind becomes relaxed and naturally settles. We need to clear away afflictions and fears, remember love and compassion, have a kind heart, and recall these instructions.

The teachings on mind training, or lojong, say that we should remember that all sentient beings have to experience the suffering of death. We think, "May this suffering not happen to any other sentient being; may all of it ripen upon me." We do the visualization of tonglen, of sending and taking, and through this we create imprints in our mind. If we do this practice in this life and create strong imprints, in the bardo these imprints will awaken and lead us toward a good rebirth. Such imprints will also awaken in that life and we will become someone who practices the Dharma more and more.

Remembering the Three Jewels and the yidam deity or doing tonglen meditation can help us when we take birth, at the time of death, and during the bardo. It is important not to be overwhelmed by the afflictions and not to be overcome by fear. Who can escort us through this? It is the lama. We ask the lama for instructions and practice them; that is how the lama guides us.

These days hospices and other services help people die comfortably without pain. These are wonderful organizations. People who are involved in such work often ask me how to help someone to die well. If the person who is dying has entered the gate of the Dharma, you can remind her about the methods of the Dharma. You can tell her to remember the Buddha, Dharma, and sangha, and to remember her meditation and yidam deities. If she can do this, it can help avert suffering at the time of death and in the bardo and help her to take a good rebirth. If the dying person does not know anything about the Dharma, it's still important for her to know about the five afflictions waiting in ambush, so that she will not be overcome by them, and to have a relaxed mind. You can encourage her to think good thoughts and to have a kind heart. If she has a relaxed mind and a kind heart as she dies, these imprints will reawaken in the bardo and when she takes her next birth.

· 25 ·

The unfailing refuge is the teacher.
Always bear the lama on your head, people of Dingri.

We need to have faith and devotion in the lama. We need to supplicate and pray to the lama. The unfailing refuge is the teacher. What does this mean? In the instructions on mahamudra, there are four types of teachers: the word lama of the sugatas or buddhas, the ultimate lama of the dharma nature, the sign lama of appearances, and the individual lama of the lineage. The first, the word lama of the sugatas, refers to the words of the Buddha, all the instructions and advice that the Buddha himself gave. This also refers to all the instructions and treatises written by the great scholars and meditation masters of India and of Tibet. All of these can free us from suffering and bring us happiness. They are important because they benefit many sentient beings.

When I began coming to North America around 1980, there was very little available on Buddhism in general and almost nothing about Vajrayana Buddhism. Later, out of compassion, many great masters came and taught. Their students developed faith and received many instructions, which they translated. Now many of the translated instructions have been made available in publications that are special and have great blessings. If you read and study them and put the instructions into practice, they are very helpful. These instructions are called the word lama of the sugatas, and you should study them well.

In the West there are many different types of books available, and not all of them require special respect or veneration. But Buddhist texts are different because they contain the instructions that can free you and all sentient beings from all of the suffering of samsara and bring the ultimate happiness of the ultimate result. You should not ignore them or regard them as unimportant. Instead, you should remember that they are truly important and wonderful, something to have faith and devotion in. Therefore, make sure never to put Dharma texts in a low place or on the floor and never to step over them. It is important to always treat Dharma texts with respect.

The second type of lama is the ultimate lama of the dharma nature. Meditation on yidam deities, tranquillity meditation, insight meditation—can we do these practices? Yes, and if we do these practices, we will be able to attain a result. There are many great masters who have given us many instructions: lojong, the preliminary and main practices, and various yidam deity practices, including peaceful and wrathful deities as well as male and female deities, and so on. There are many instructions and meditations. If we practice these instructions, we can achieve the ultimate result. The ability to achieve the ultimate result is known as the ultimate lama of the dharma nature.

The third type of lama is the sign lama of appearances. As Milarepa said:

> I take all that appears and exists as a text;
> I've never studied texts in ink.

In order to understand, for example, impermanence, it is not necessary to listen to lamas' explanations or to study texts. Milarepa's taking appearance and existence as his texts means just looking at samsara, seeing what this world of samsara is like, and knowing it for ourselves. Suffering and impermanence can be observed directly this way.

These days we have televisions, and when we watch the news on CNN or the BBC, what do we see? In one location, there is a war and many people are suffering. Then we see a segment about a blazing wildfire that is burning down homes and creating great difficulties. The next piece is about a lake or river that is flooding and causing destruction. Next there's been an earthquake that has brought about all sorts of devastation. We can see that everything is impermanent and there is suffering. We need to free ourselves from this suffering. The way to free ourselves is to practice the Dharma, pray to the Three Jewels, and make aspirations. This is the sign lama of appearances. It means that if we look, we can see how things are.

The fourth type of lama is the individual lama of the lineage. The Buddha gave instructions that have been passed from one individual to the next in an uninterrupted line of lamas. Our Kagyu teachings originated from the dharmakaya Vajradhara, who transmitted them to Tilopa, and from him to Naropa, and so on through a series of the great masters down to our root lama, the glorious Seventeenth Karmapa, Ogyen Trinley Dorje. Each of them is the individual lama of the lineage to whom we can pray and supplicate.

What do we need in a spiritual friend? In *The Jewel Ornament of Liberation,* Gampopa wrote that there are four types of spiritual friend: the spiritual friend who is the sambhogakaya of the Buddha, the spiritual friend who is a supreme nirmanakaya, the spiritual friend who is a bodhisattva dwelling on a high level, and the spiritual friend who is an ordinary individual. Which of these spiritual friends is most important? The most important is the lama who is an ordinary individual. We may not have the karma or the fortune to be able to meet lamas who are on the sambhogakaya, supreme nirmanakaya, or high bodhisattva levels. But we do have the fortune to be able to meet lamas who are ordinary individuals and to receive the Dharma from them. We can ask for and receive instructions, and it is important to do so with faith and devotion.

Generally the lamas' instructions in our Karma Kagyu tradition are the main practices of mahamudra and the Six Yogas of Naropa, and we usually do them in order. We start with the common preliminaries followed by the special preliminaries, then the instructions on mind training, and then the creation stage of visualizing yidam deities and the completion stage. During the completion stage, we alternate between mahamudra and the Six Yogas of Naropa. We follow this progression.

In Tibet we did these practices in one retreat lasting three years and three fortnights or phases of the moon. These days you have to do them in a way that suits your particular time and place. Sometimes it's not possible to sit a long retreat; it just doesn't fit with your life. If a lama were to say, "Unless you can do a three-year retreat, you cannot practice Dharma at all; you'll miss your opportunity," that is a sign that the lama is not taking proper care of you. These traditional practices are helpful, and doing them in sequence is important, but they should be done in a way that does not cause harm in your life. When the lama gives you instructions, you can follow them in a way that fits with your life. If you can complete all the practices in one retreat, that would be wonderful. But not everyone has the fortune to be able to do that. If you can gradually do a few of the practices, that would be very beneficial.

You need the lama to teach you the instructions and to give them in a way that you can actually carry out. This is what Padampa Sangye means when he says to always bear the lama on your head. If you practice the Dharma in this way, relying on the lama's instructions, you will not be led astray. Following them is very important.

٭ 26 ٭

Your protection is the lama; rouse devotion
As your fare and you'll get where you want to go, people of Dingri.

The lama gives us instructions, and when we receive them, we need to have faith in and believe what the lama says. You may have read that the lama is similar to the Buddha or even superior to the Buddha. You might wonder why. The lama may not seem like a buddha. Lamas sometimes have faults, and if they do, do you have to pretend that they have no faults? When it is said that the lama is superior to the Buddha, does it mean that the lama has qualities that surpass the Buddha's qualities? If the lama lacks enlightened qualities, does that mean that you have to pretend otherwise? No, that's not what it means.

The lama may have faults. The lama may lack qualities. You should not follow lamas because they have all the qualities and no faults. This is not about lamas who are not made of flesh and blood, whose body is made of radiant light that fills the sky! The lama is not someone who never gets sick or suffers. The lama does get sick and does have problems. The lama gets hungry and has to eat. The lama gets thirsty and has to drink. It's not as though we need a lama who never feels pangs of hunger or thirst.

What do we need from the lama? We need someone who can give us the instructions that come from the Buddha and from the dharmakaya Vajradhara. If we have faith, devotion, and belief in the instructions, they can take us where we need to go. Practicing them will free us from the suffering of samsara and bring happiness and the ultimate result. If we can't practice them, we can't practice them. Since practicing them will free us, we should have faith and devotion in these instructions.

✦ 27 ✦

People who have riches end up stingy.
Give to others without any bias, people of Dingri.

If we have some wealth or material things, often we get miserly at the same time. We need to give to others without bias. If we can give with a good heart, even just a little bit, it is very important to do so. If we have wealth and material things, we need to put them to use in ways that will help others and ourselves, and we need to do this impartially.

✦ 28 ✦

People who have power turn to evil.
Humbly place your fingers on your chest, people of Dingri.

When we have power and influence, there is a danger of using them to commit misdeeds or to harm others. As Nagarjuna said:

> Desire, aversion, and delusion—
> These three produce unvirtuous acts.

There is the danger of acting that way when we gain power. What do we need to do about this? We need to place our ten fingers on our chest as a sincere gesture of examining what we have done. Is our action good or bad? If it is good, that is fortunate, perhaps even wonderful. If it is wrong, we need to make sure it does not happen again.

People often ask me how to prevent feeling a lot of anger and how to deal with emotions. The main instruction for dealing with such problems is to take afflictions as the path. If your meditation is strong, you will be able to do this, but if not, it is difficult to take afflictions as the path. Ordinary individuals need a method to decrease the afflictions. Here is the way to do this.

When you wake up in the morning, tell yourself, "When I get angry, I do things that harm myself and others. Even if I don't want this to happen, it still occurs. In order to make sure it doesn't happen, today I am making a commitment to maintain mindfulness and awareness so that I will not get angry. If nonetheless I do get angry, I will not act on it."

Make this commitment in the morning, and then in the evening say to yourself, "This morning I made a commitment to be mindful and aware, not get angry, and not act on anger. How did it go?" If it went well, think, "This is good; I kept my commitment. I'm going to make the same commitment tomorrow." If it didn't go well, tell yourself, "I got angry and broke my commitment. That wasn't good. Tomorrow I'm going to make the same commitment and redouble my efforts to be mindful and aware. I'm going to make sure this does not happen again."

Do this every day. It is quite possible that there will be days when you get angry. There might even be a period when you get angry every day. This is natural for us ordinary individuals, and there is no need to be afraid or to think you can't do this or to give up. Just keep doing it every day. Make the commitment in the morning and evaluate it in the evening. Keep your mindfulness and awareness. If you do this every day, gradually the afflictions will diminish. This is what is meant when Padampa Sangye says that you need to humbly place your fingers on your chest. You need to examine yourself, to look at what you have been doing.

* 29 *

In this human world, there are no friends or family.
Place your confidence in Dharma, people of Dingri.

What does it mean to say that in this human world there are no friends or family? Of course we have friends and family. But the great bodhisattva Shantideva said that the characteristic of ordinary individuals is that they strive for their own benefit and do not generally work for the benefit of others. Friends and family here means people who work for others' benefit, people who work to help us. We ordinary individuals are all working for our own benefit, striving for our own selfish ends. People like this, even if they live together, don't really become friends. For that reason it doesn't make sense to lose ourselves to attachment and fixation on such people, because they're just trying to benefit themselves. In what can we place our confidence? We should place our confidence in the Dharma. We should encourage others to practice the Dharma, and we need to accomplish the Dharma ourselves. If we do this, we will bring benefit to both ourselves and others.

· 30 ·

Precious human life is wasted through distraction.
Act decisively right now, people of Dingri.

If we get distracted, we eventually find ourselves in circumstances in which we are not able to practice the Dharma. Do we presently have the support that will allow us to accomplish the Dharma? Yes, we have it. Do we have the opportunity to practice the Dharma? We have the wonderful opportunity to practice. If we practice and accomplish the Dharma and benefit ourselves, that is very fortunate. If we do not practice the Dharma and instead let ourselves get distracted, we will lose this opportunity and waste the freedoms and advantages of human life. We therefore need to make the decision to practice Dharma now. We need to decrease the afflictions at once and not act out misdeeds and nonvirtues. It is important to practice taking up virtue and giving up nonvirtue right away. In this way, we need to act decisively right now.

· 31 ·

While you are distracted, death will seize you.
Practice from this very moment on, people of Dingri.

Padampa Sangye gave this advice to encourage us to practice the Dharma with diligence and to counteract distractedness. Why do we get distracted? We get distracted because of clinging to permanence. Thinking our lives will last for a long time, we become attached to worldly activities, our mind gets distracted, and we don't practice the Dharma. Yet there is the danger that in the interim impermanence will strike and we will die. In order to urge us to practice the Dharma now, Padampa Sangye talks a lot about impermanence. This is easy to understand.

We become attached to our wealth and possessions, to food and clothing, to our home—all the good things in life. Through clinging to these things, we get distracted. We might have faith in the Dharma and understand that we need to practice it, but we are so distracted that we don't get around to it. Even though we understand death and impermanence, and we know that death is going to happen to us, distractedness makes us lazy. This is a difficult situation. The verse is an exhortation to practice the Dharma now—from this very moment onward. Don't take your time getting around to Dharma practice. Do it right now.

* 32 *

Who knows when the demon Death will come?
Now you need to stand on your own two feet, people of Dingri.

Death is like a demon—powerful, awesome, and fearsome. We don't know with certainty when the demon of death will catch us. If we knew when our death was coming, then we could make a plan to enjoy worldly pleasures for a little while and then practice the Dharma later, but we can't plan our lives in that way because we don't actually know when the demon Death will come. It could be in a few years, or it might be a long time from now. Or death could come suddenly—we don't know. If our death doesn't come for a long time, that's good. But if it happens now, when we haven't done anything to prepare for it through the Dharma, then this human life would be wasted. We would not have done anything meaningful, and we would have lost the chance for our future lives as well. So we need to act now. Knowing that we have begun to practice the Dharma and prepare for death gives some peace of mind. Then we know that in the future we will be able to reach the ultimate result. Therefore it's important to practice the Dharma right now.

⁺ 33 ⁺

When you die, there's no one to protect you.
You can only count upon yourselves, people of Dingri.

Who can protect you from death? Whom can you count on when you die? Can an extremely wealthy, influential person protect you when you are on your deathbed? Can an incredibly powerful person, a five-star general, protect you when you are stricken with a fatal illness? No. No matter how much wealth or worldly power people may have, they cannot protect you.

But there is someone who can protect you in this situation: you can protect yourself by practicing the Dharma. In the best of circumstances, as a result of your Dharma practice, you can gain control over your rebirth. But even if that doesn't happen, you can say to yourself, "I did my Dharma practice diligently, and now I have no fear of death. I'm not afraid of falling into the lower realms in my next life." At the very least you'll be able to think, "I did some Dharma practice, and this is good. I was diligent about it, and the results of this will not be lost in the future." Even if you are not able to do a great deal of Dharma practice but only a small amount, you can know that it will have a beneficial result and will not be lost. In this way, you can count on yourself.

⁺ 34 ⁺

Like the shadows lengthening at sunset,
Demon Death inexorably comes closer.
Quickly, quickly, run away from him, people of Dingri.

In the evening, as the sun sets, it sinks lower in the sky, and the shadows get longer and longer. At first the shadows are small and far from us, but they don't stay still. They keep coming closer and closer. Similarly, the demon Death inexorably comes closer—death and impermanence don't stay still; they come closer and closer.

"Quickly, quickly, run away from him!" How do we run away from the demon Death? We need a way to liberate ourselves from death. The best method is to free ourselves from samsara and the lower realms. Until we are able to do that, for the short term, we can supplicate Amitayus or Green Tara. If we visualize ourselves as Amitayus or Green Tara, recite their mantras, and perform the practices, they can help us avert an untimely death. Will these practices keep death away from us forever? No, but they can help prevent our dying prematurely, and therefore these practices are very helpful.

◈ 35 ◈

Flowers bloom today and wilt tomorrow.
Don't place any trust in your own body, people of Dingri.

A flower might be beautiful, colorful, and vivid, but it doesn't last for very long—a few days or a week, and then it wilts and dies. The body is the same. We might be young, beautiful, and strong, but illness and aging and death will eventually come. Our body isn't stable. As Padampa Sangye says, "Don't place any trust in your own body"—no matter how nice, eventually our body will decay. This is why we need to strive at the Dharma now. The Dharma is what can protect us.

To protect ourselves from sickness in the short term, we can pray to and do the practice of Medicine Buddha. This is very helpful for freeing the body of pain, helping us recover from illness more quickly, and making our medical treatment more effective. If we are healthy, it can help maintain our good health for a long time. In terms of lasting benefit, we need to attain the ultimate result of the Dharma, to free ourselves from samsara. But for the short term, meditating on the Medicine Buddha, reciting his mantra, and supplicating him is very beneficial.

Another practice to increase our life force and merit is saving the lives of beings through life releases. We are fearful about our own death, and so are animals. Fish and animals and insects all cherish their own lives; they do not want to die any more than we do. When they face the prospect of death—whether they sicken, are attacked by other animals, or suddenly get killed—they experience fear and great suffering. Therefore, one of the best ways to accumulate merit is to perform a life-release ceremony according to the methods taught by the buddhas and bodhisattvas of the past. This not only brings the temporary benefit of rescuing the animals that we release, but there are also the benefits that are called liberation through seeing, liberation through tasting, liberation through hearing, and so forth. These are also very helpful for those animals.

For liberation through seeing during the life-release ceremony, we show beings a small statue of the Buddha or pictures of yidam deities. Of course, fish and animals and insects cannot actually practice the Dharma; they can't meditate or pray or recite mantras, and they don't normally have any opportunity to see a statue of the Buddha. But during a life release, if we show them a statue of the Buddha, it can help them. Does this liberate them immediately and erase all their suffering in an instant? No, but it creates an imprint. From the beginning of samsara until now, they have not had an opportunity to see an image of the Buddha. Seeing an image of the Buddha plants a small seed in their mind streams. This seed will gradually grow and grow, and eventually it will lead to liberation from samsara.

Liberation through tasting is similar. In this case, we give blessed nectar or pills to the beings. When they taste these, the animals receive their blessings and their power, which again creates a dharmic imprint. It is a small virtuous imprint, which is a cause for attaining liberation from samsara in the future. This is a great benefit for the animals and excellent merit for us. Performing life-release ceremonies will help us remain healthy, improve illnesses, and become happy in this life, which will help us reach the ultimate result. We must not place our trust in our own body. We need to put our hopes in Dharma practice.

· 36 ·

Like the children of the gods while living,
Fearsome as a mob of demons dead—
Your illusory bodies have you tricked, people of Dingri.

We have a strong attachment to our own body. We cherish it, but this does not actually help us. One day something will go wrong with our body. No matter how beautiful our body is while we are alive, the day we die, it becomes a corpse. As a corpse, it's completely horrifying, and no one wants it. So we see that there is no essence to the body. Our illusory body has us tricked.

In order not to be fooled by our body, we need to put it to use for the Dharma, as Shantideva said. This benefits us and others. For example, the Buddha appeared in the world, attained perfect buddhahood, and turned the wheel of Dharma; through this he helped countless sentient beings by bringing them to the ultimate state of liberation and omniscience. Likewise, many extraordinary masters have appeared and taught the Dharma; they helped many others and also freed themselves from samsara's vast ocean of suffering. They did this by using their body well to practice generosity, discipline, patience, and the other paramitas. In particular, there have been many masters of the Vajrayana who have used their body in this way and attained a good result.

As Shantideva said, "Use the body as a boat to cross to the other side of the ocean of samsara. And when you come to the other side, leave the boat behind." We are on the shores of the great ocean of samsara, the ocean of suffering. In order to free ourselves from these waters, we need something to bring us across. We need a boat, and that boat is our body. We need to use our body well, and if we do, we can free ourselves from samsara. But if we are tricked by our attachment to this illusory body, we'll forget to do so.

* 37 *

Business done, the market goers scatter.
Friends are sure to leave you in the end, people of Dingri.

It is very good, of course, to care for our friends and relatives and to have love and compassion for them. But when attachment to them becomes an obstacle to our practicing the Dharma, this does not help us or them. Similarly, we need to be sure that we do not create obstacles for others, and we need to be diligent about this.

We may be with our friends and relatives now, but how long will it last? We think that we will be together for a long time, but will it be for hundreds or thousands of years? No. We are not going to be around that long, nor are they. It's like people coming together at a market or for a conference. They come to do their business and stay a few days or a week or a month, but when their business is done, they go home. In the same way, we need to make sure that we accomplish what we need to, and being too attached to others is not going to help. Why? Friends are sure to leave you in the end. Someday we will have to leave, and someday our friends and relatives will have to leave. In these circumstances, we can help ourselves by acting in ways that fit with the Dharma, by practicing and generating love and compassion. Being attached does not help in any way.

* 38 *

The illusory scarecrows that you build are sure to topple,
So now get ready something that you'll never lose, people of Dingri.

Our body has no essence, like a scarecrow. Even if it's well made, eventually it's going to fall apart. It cannot bring any lasting benefit. What can bring us lasting benefit is the practice of the Dharma. If we can do excellent Dharma practice, that is best, but even if we do only a little Dharma practice, that places the seed of liberation within us. That seed will grow and ultimately free us from all the suffering of samsara.

• 39 •

Mind is an eagle, sure to fly away.
Now's the time to soar up to the skies, people of Dingri.

We have a body and a mind, and it seems like our mind resides within our body; the mind clings to the body as a self. But is it going to remain this way for long? It is not. The mind is like an eagle. An eagle stays happily in its nest for a while, but at some point it is sure to fly away. In the same way, the mind resides in the body, but eventually it has to leave. We need to make sure that when the mind leaves the body, it has a good place to go. Just as an eagle needs a place to fly to, we need a good destination. For this purpose, we need to practice the Dharma.

In light of this, what is most helpful to do with our body, speech, and mind? The great masters and the buddhas and bodhisattvas have given many useful instructions. Perhaps we think, "If only I could be reborn in a pure land with a beautiful body in a lovely place surrounded by lotuses. How wonderful!" Is it possible for us to be born in a pure land? Yes, it is possible because the buddha Amitabha made the great compassionate aspiration that anyone who has the four causes for rebirth in his pure realm, the realm of Sukhavati, can be reborn there. Although there are many other pure realms, for the most part only bodhisattvas who have attained the levels can be reborn in those realms. But ordinary individuals, if they have the four causes for rebirth there, can be reborn in the realm of Sukhavati.

The first of the four causes is to think about the realm of Sukhavati: imagine it, remember it, repeatedly bring it to mind. Think that in this realm there is the great buddha Amitabha, and he is surrounded by all the great buddhas and bodhisattvas and in particular by the bodhisattvas Avalokiteshvara and Vajrapani. Actually visualize them there and recite an aspiration prayer for rebirth in Sukhavati.[4] We recite this in order to bring the pure realm of Sukhavati to mind, thinking, "This is what the pure land is like. I'm going there." Imagining the pure realm of Sukhavati in our mind is the first cause for being reborn there.

The second cause is to gather the accumulation of merit. There are many wonderful ways that we can accumulate merit using our body, speech, and mind. With our body, we can offer prostrations. With our speech, we can recite mantras. With our mind, we can practice deep samadhi and meditate on love, compassion, and bodhichitta. We can also use our possessions and our wealth to make offerings to the buddhas and the Three Jewels and to make gifts to the downtrodden. In terms of practice, often the best way to accumulate merit is through what is known as the seven-branch prayer. The seven branches are to prostrate, make offerings, make confessions, rejoice in the virtue of others, request the buddhas to turn the wheel of Dharma, supplicate the buddhas and bodhisattvas not to pass into nirvana, and dedicate the virtue to the benefit of others. Accumulating merit by means such as the seven-branch prayer is the second cause for rebirth in Amitabha's pure realm of Sukhavati.

The third cause is to develop the resolve of bodhichitta. All sentient beings, who are as limitless as space and who have all been our mothers at some point in the past, have fallen into suffering. They don't even recognize it as suffering but confuse it with happiness. They are overpowered by karma and the afflictions. Realizing this, we think, "I need to practice in order to help these beings." That is bodhichitta, the third cause.

The fourth cause is to make an aspiration. We dedicate all the virtue that we and all others have performed as a cause for rebirth in the pure realms and then make the aspiration: "Through this virtue, may all sentient beings be born in the pure realm."

You might think that cultivating these four causes seems very difficult. Or you could think, "I can actually do that. It's not so hard." And now is the time to do it! Like an eagle, you have to practice soaring in the sky now so that your mind will have a good place to go.

⋄ 40 ⋄

For your kindly parents, beings of the six realms,
Cultivate love, cultivate compassion, people of Dingri.

We need to free ourselves and others from the suffering of samsara. If at first we have the limited motivation of trying to free only ourselves from suffering, this is all right, though it's a bit small-minded to think just of ourselves. Over time, all our former parents in the six realms of samsara have been kind and affectionate to us. If we don't think of them, we are not repaying their kindness in any way. Maybe it's fine to think only of ourselves, yet it's somewhat shameful to think in that way.

We should genuinely try to view all sentient beings with love and compassion. Through this there will be times when we can actually bring beings the happiness that they wish for and free them from suffering. This is wonderful. Even if we aren't able to do that, we can at least meditate on having a kind heart. Meditating on having a kind heart may not help others right away, but with the right motivation, we will eventually have an opportunity to help them.

In the Mahayana tradition, it is taught that we need to develop and increase our love and compassion for all the beings of the six realms of samsara from the start. Why? From beginningless time, all these sentient beings have been our parents and cared for us. They have been loving, compassionate, and kind to us, and so we need to meditate on love and compassion for them. As it says, "Cultivate love, cultivate compassion." Meditating on love and compassion will generate great merit for us, but the benefit is not just for us; in the future a vast benefit will also come to other sentient beings.

When we meditate on love and compassion, we need to be unbiased and impartial. Generally, there is nothing wrong with meditating on love and compassion for our friends and families, but it is better to meditate without that sort of partiality. That is why Padampa Sangye says that we should meditate on love and compassion toward all the beings of the six realms, who have been our parents.

Among the Dharma instructions for increasing love and compassion, there are the teachings on cultivating the four immeasurables: immeasurable love, immeasurable compassion, immeasurable joy, and immeasurable equanimity. Recitation of these begins, "May all sentient beings have happiness and its cause," which is the meditation on love. Then, to meditate on compassion, we say, "May all sentient beings be free of suffering and its cause." Followed by the next two, this is the usual order. However, in *The Words of My Perfect Teacher,* the great lama Patrul Rinpoche taught that we should meditate first on equanimity. If we start by meditating on love and compassion, there is the danger of becoming biased in the meditations. We need to make sure that doesn't happen. If we think about a friend or an enemy, we should meditate without feeling attachment toward the friend or aversion toward the enemy, and for that reason we must meditate on equanimity. We meditate until we see all sentient beings equally. Then we meditate on loving-kindness, which is the wish to bring beings happiness, and then we meditate on compassion, the wish to free them from suffering. This approach will bring a good result.

◦ 41 ◦

Foes are karmic misperceptions of samsara.
Cast off viciousness and hatred, people of Dingri.

We need to meditate upon love and compassion. What prevents us from having love and compassion? Mainly it is the afflictions such as hatred, jealousy, and so forth. We need to learn how to give up hatred and the wish to harm.

Sometimes it seems as though we have hostile enemies, people who harm us and get in our way. This is just a karmic misperception of samsara—just the confused appearances of samsara. They appear in this life because of our actions in previous lives. Therefore, we have to practice patience. When we have someone to practice patience for, we can gather a lot of virtue and thereby complete the accumulation of merit. This is actually the best way to gather merit. As Shantideva said in *The Way of the Bodhisattva*, "There is no austerity like patience."

It is very difficult to practice patience because it is hard to find an object with whom to practice. If we want to practice generosity, for example, there are beggars everywhere. There is always someone to whom we can be generous. But it's much more difficult to find enemies—people who get angry at us, who hurt us—with whom we have to be patient. If we don't do anything to harm someone else, then no one does anything to harm us in return. Since Dharma practitioners generally don't harm anyone, no one does anything mean to us in return, so we often can't find people to practice patience with. When we do, it is a wonderful support for our Dharma practice. So-called enemies are merely confused, samsaric misperceptions, so we need to cast off our viciousness and hatred and practice patience.

In order to do this, we need to know the reasons for doing it. Among the many texts and treatises, chapter 6 of *The Way of the Bodhisattva* by Shantideva clearly explains the way to practice patience. This chapter is helpful for recognizing whom one needs to practice patience with and the benefits of practicing patience.

+ 42 +

Refuge and reciting mantras purify
Speech's obscurations; give up idle talk, people of Dingri.

When we practice the secret mantra Vajrayana, we recite mantras, and usually this is done along with samadhi meditation. Reciting a mantra is important for purifying our misdeeds and obscurations of speech. The mantra of any deity is good to recite.

Reciting the refuge prayer is also important. There are different ways to take refuge. The general way of taking refuge, common to all Buddhist traditions, is to go for refuge to the Three Jewels: to the Buddha as the teacher, the Dharma as the path, and the sangha as our companions on the path.

In the tradition of the secret mantra Vajrayana, we have the special fourfold refuge: in addition to going for refuge to the Three Jewels, we go for refuge to the root lama and lineage lamas, due to whose kindness we are able to receive Dharma instructions. In taking the fourfold refuge, we say, "I go for refuge to the glorious lamas. I go for refuge to the Buddha. I go for refuge to the Dharma. I go for refuge to the Sangha."

In the secret mantra Vajrayana, we also have the sixfold refuge. In addition to going for refuge to the Three Jewels, we also go for refuge to the three roots: to the lama, the root of blessings; to the yidam deities, the root of accomplishment; and to the Dharma protectors, the root of activity. This is the sixfold refuge for the particular practices of the Vajrayana.

The lama is called the root of blessings. What do we mean by blessings? Sometimes people think that receiving blessings means that you start to tremble, see all sorts of colors and lights, have fantastic visions, and so on. But that is not what blessings do. Blessings actually bring out the power of the Dharma. If you have only a little faith in the Dharma, your faith increases. If you have only a little devotion to the Dharma, your devotion increases. If you have only a little wisdom, your wisdom increases.

When our mind turns toward the Dharma, we wish to practice it. Because of this wish, we practice, and because we practice, we can attain the ultimate result. This is the meaning of blessings: the power of the Dharma. Blessings come from the lama.

Of course, the blessings of the Dharma originally come from the Buddha, but we do not have the fortune to meet the Buddha and listen to him teach the Dharma in his own voice. However, this is not a problem. Through the compassion of the Buddha, we are still cared for. We can receive all of the power and blessings from the root and lineage lamas just as we would have from the Buddha himself. For this reason the lama is the root of blessings.

The second of the three roots is the root of accomplishment, the yidam deities. In terms of the common refuge, the Dharma is the path. But there are eighty-four thousand different types of Dharma, and we cannot practice them all, nor do we need to. We only need to practice the ones that match our present capabilities, so we do the practices for which we feel the most faith and devotion.

The yidam deities are the meditation deities to whom we make a mental commitment to practice. This is the meaning of the Tibetan word *yidam,* from *yi* (mind)and *dam* (commitment). We might do the practice of one or two or any number of deities for whom we feel the most faith and devotion. By practicing what are known as the creation phase and completion phase of the yidam according to the oral instructions, we can come to accomplish the actual result. In this way, the yidam deities are the root of accomplishment.

Third is the root of activity, the Dharma protector. Sometimes we encounter difficulties and obstacles in practicing the Dharma. Obstacles arise when we start losing faith, devotion, diligence, or confidence. To free ourselves from such difficulties and gain the necessary favorable conditions, we need a companion who can help us. In terms of the common refuge, the sangha is our companion. The sangha is composed of the individuals who give us the instructions that help us increase our faith and our diligence. They are human beings whom we can actually encounter, and they become our companions on the path.

There are also many buddhas and bodhisattvas who dwell in the invisible expanse. Even though we cannot see them directly, they can help us eliminate our difficulties and gather favorable conditions. When we supplicate them, they can appear in the form of Dharma protectors, who help us through the compassion and power of all the buddhas and bodhisattvas. If we supplicate the Dharma protectors and exhort them to perform their activities, they can help free us from difficulties and help us accomplish what we need to. For example, in the Mahakala practice, we invoke the activity of the protectors, supplicate them, and offer them tormas. Because of this, they can help eliminate obstacles and gather all the conditions we need.

When we look at depictions of the Dharma protectors, they often have a wrathful, fierce, and even frightening appearance. This is actually a sign of the compassionate power of their mind. Out of great compassion, they made the aspiration to free all sentient beings from suffering and bring them to happiness. Seeing that sentient beings have been overcome by the afflictions, they are unable to bear it, so they have this wrathful appearance. Fundamentally it is not anger but a sign of the strength of their compassion. When you look at a painting of Mahakala, at first glance he looks very wrathful and threatening, but if you look carefully, Mahakala is laughing. This is the strength of Mahakala's compassion. When we do this practice to invoke the activity of Mahakala and the Dharma protectors, we offer tormas and golden libation and supplicate them to help us practice the Dharma properly without obstacles. In this way, the Dharma protectors are the root of activity, which has real benefit and power.

In this verse, Padampa Sangye also says, "Give up idle talk, people of Dingri." We talk constantly. Sometimes our ordinary conversation has meaning and purpose, but sometimes it is pointless. Such pointless talk not only wastes time, but it also gradually increases our hostility and anger, jealousy, and delusion. It is a cause for increasing the afflictions, which then leads us to wrong action; we accumulate bad karma, and this harms us as well as others. We therefore need to give up idle, pointless conversation.

* 43 *

Circumambulation and prostration purify
Bodily obscurations; give up worldly actions, people of Dingri.

By doing prostrations and circumambulations, we are using our body to gather merit, which helps purify all the obscurations of the body. Then, Padampa Sangye says, "Give up worldly actions." If our worldly physical actions are done with a kind heart, with the wish to help, with altruism and love and compassion, there is nothing wrong with that. But worldly actions that are done with a sense of competitiveness or jealousy or out of hatred or malice are harmful to us and to others, and ultimately a bad result will ripen on us alone.

◦ 44 ◦

Fierce devotion purifies your mental habits.
Visualize the lama on your crown, people of Dingri.

Devotion is extremely important. But devotion does not develop just from being told, "This is important; you should have devotion for it." The Dharma is something that we practice. If we actually put it into practice, we can free ourselves from karma and the afflictions and thereby free ourselves from suffering. In order to do that, we need strong belief in the Dharma.

If we have strong belief in the Dharma, we will be able to practice fully and wholeheartedly. If we have 100 percent conviction, we will practice 100 percent. If our conviction is 50 percent, our practice will be 50 percent. If our conviction is only 10 percent, then our practice will be only 10 percent. The more devotion we have, the better we will be able to practice. If our practice is good, we will be able to purify our mental habits, which will bring great benefit.

This is why Padampa Sangye says, "Visualize the lama on your crown." Where do the instructions come from? They come from the lama, so imagine the lama above the crown of your head as a reminder of how important and beneficial the lama's instructions are.

◦ 45 ◦

The flesh and bones you're born with all will come apart.
Do not cling to life as if it were eternal, people of Dingri.

This verse is about impermanence. When we were born, our bones, flesh, and internal organs had all been formed together. But, at the time of our death, they will come apart. The flesh will come off the bones; the bones themselves will separate; our body will come apart completely. We should not expect to live an extremely long life and make plans to spend hundreds or thousands of years doing worldly things. Thinking in that way is not helpful at all. Do not cling to life as if it were eternal.

In terms of the preliminary practices and the actual practice, up to this point Padampa Sangye has been addressing the preliminaries. In terms of the relative and the ultimate, up to this point we have been discussing primarily relative appearances—why we need to practice, develop diligence, and so on. Now we have come to the actual practice. In the actual practice, in terms of relative appearances and the ultimate, Padampa Sangye primarily talks about the ultimate. Later on, in the section on the enhancement of the practice, there is more discussion of the relative.

* 46 *

Grasp the finest object, your own constant nature,
Which is free of change and fluctuation, people of Dingri.

We use phrases like "awaken to buddhahood" and "achieve accomplishment," but what do they actually mean? Do they mean that we have to get rid of everything old and make something new? Do they mean we have to go someplace far away? No, they do not.

Our mind has confused perceptions. From these confused perceptions, various appearances occur. We cling to a "me," a self, and through clinging to a self, we experience all the afflictions. Acting under the power of the afflictions, we accumulate karma. Karma causes us to experience even more confused perceptions of samsara. We need a way to free ourselves from this cycle. The way to free ourselves is not to look far away, but rather to turn inward, to come back to ourselves, and to look at our actual nature—the finest object, our own constant nature. "Nature" here refers to an unchanged or unaltered state.

From the perspective of the Foundation Vehicle, this is called the selflessness of the individual. There is not really any "me." The nature of samsara is suffering. The root of samsara comes down to the afflictions: greed, aversion, delusion, and so on. The root of the afflictions is clinging to a sense of "me." We think, "I exist; I am here," and because we think, "I'm here," we think, "That's nice; I want something good"—we develop greed. We think, "That hurts; I don't want that"—we develop aversion or hatred. We think, "That other person is doing better than I am"—we develop envy. What happens when we develop these afflictions? Because of the afflictions, we perform actions and accumulate karma. Since these are not good actions but bad actions, we reap their result, which is suffering. The root of all this is clinging to a self. We need to eliminate clinging to a self. But how? We cannot simply decide, "From now on I'm going to give up clinging to a self."

In the nature of reality, is there really a self? We think that the self exists and it is either the body or the mind. Is the body the self? We have a head, arms and legs, eyes and ears, and all the rest. Are any of these a self? No. We think that there is a singular, solid thing that is the self, but the body is just a collection of parts, an aggregate of all these things put together.

There are five kinds of aggregates, which are collections of many things brought together. They have a continuum, but there isn't really anything there. For that reason, there is no real self at all. Since we have not realized this, we cling to the idea of a self. If we know that in reality there is no self, our clinging to a self will be naturally pacified and subdued. When it is subdued, we can give up the afflictions and thereby free ourselves of suffering forever. This is the path of the Foundation Vehicle.

The Mahayana sutras on the prajnaparamita teach not only the selflessness of the individual but that all phenomena are naturally empty. This is taught in the most concise form in the *Heart Sutra,* which says, "no form, no sound, no smell, no taste, no touch, no dharmas," and so forth. Everything is empty in essence, and that empty essence is the nature of all things. All things are naturally nonexistent; they are emptiness. If we know everything as naturally empty, we will not experience suffering or the afflictions. The afflictions and suffering are also naturally empty. Having seen that the confused appearances of samsara are essentially empty, we can then grasp the finest object, the constant natural state.

The *Heart Sutra* teaches simply that all phenomena are emptiness. The treatises on the Middle Way by Nagarjuna, Chandrakirti,

Shantarakshita, Shantideva, and others teach the logical arguments that prove why external appearances are empty and why our internal perceiving mind is empty. Reading these texts is extremely helpful for developing certainty that all phenomena are emptiness. They are of the Mahayana tradition.

In our own special tradition of the secret mantra Vajrayana, we don't examine whether external phenomena are empty or not. The nature of the mind is the basis of everything, as is taught in the songs of great masters such as Saraha, Naropa, and Tilopa. We need to see this nature of the mind. Whether we are talking about the appearances of samsara or the strong afflictions, there is no change or fluctuation in the nature of mind in terms of its nature. If we try to meditate on this, we can. And we can see that the nature of everything is essentially unchanging.

* 47 *

Use the finest jewel, the mind's own nature.
This great wealth will never get depleted, people of Dingri.

We want happiness and to enjoy life, so we accumulate wealth and possessions. Yet material wealth eventually gets used up. But there is the finest jewel, a great wealth that will never get depleted. What is it? It is our mind. If we understand the nature of the mind, it is the supreme wealth that can bring us great happiness.

According to the instructions of the Vajrayana, if we know what the nature of the mind is like, we can enjoy the great wealth of the mind. We know that all phenomena are emptiness, and therefore external phenomena cannot harm us in any way. The root of all happiness is the mind; the root of all suffering is the mind. The root of all afflictions and the root of all faith, devotion, love, and compassion come down to the mind. If we know the nature of our mind, we can make use of this great treasure and eventually gain perfect happiness and the ultimate result of liberation and omniscience.

The masters of India—Saraha, Tilopa, Naropa, and all of the eighty-four mahasiddhas—were great meditators, both men and women, who gave extraordinary instructions on ascertaining and recognizing the nature of the mind. These are instructions for attaining the result in one lifetime with one body, and by following these instructions and practicing them, we can attain it, whether we are male or female. Doing so is enjoying the inexhaustible treasure of the nature of mind. If we put this to use, not only can we practice, but we can achieve limitless and unchanging happiness free of any fault caused by impermanence. We need to practice and use the nature of the mind that never gets depleted.

These days many wonderful lamas have come to the West and given pointing-out instructions on the nature of the mind, and many fine students have recognized this and benefited greatly from it. When we recognize the nature of the mind through a pointing-out instruction, in terms of view, meditation, and conduct, this is the view. It is a view that comes not from inference and reasoning but from direct perception. This is excellent, but it is not complete. It is just a view—it needs to be nurtured in meditation. Nurturing this view in our meditation is what is meant by using the finest treasure, the mind's own nature. We need to meditate.

· 48 ·

Taste the finest food, samadhi's flavor.
It will soothe the pangs of hunger, people of Dingri.

How do we nurture the view in meditation? It is similar to the way we take care of our body. In order to nurture our body and keep it healthy and strong, we need good food and drink. We need to eat nutritious food that has a lot of protein and vitamins.

As in that analogy, we need food for our meditation to improve. What type of good food do we need? We need to meditate in samadhi. First we do tranquillity and insight meditation, and then we recognize the nature of mind. We need what Padampa Sangye called the finest object, the natural state, and the finest jewel, the mind's own nature. First we need to recognize and know them. Then we need to nurture them, examine how well we know them, and practice meditation. To do that, we need samadhi.

The Sanskrit word *samadhi* is translated into Tibetan as *tingdzin,* which literally means "deep holding." The mind is held firmly and deeply so the meditation becomes very stable. Samadhi can refer to either tranquillity meditation or insight meditation. By doing this deep meditation, we experience the flavor of samadhi—the exquisite taste of meditation. Through tasting it, we can attain a wonderful result, as we can see from the examples of the eighty-four great mahasiddhas of India. In Tibet, the special instructions of the Kagyu lineage—mahamudra, which was taught by the Buddha in the *King of Samadhi Sutra* and passed down to Gampopa—are able to produce experience. Through those instructions, meditators can taste the finest food, samadhi's flavor.

This flavor of samadhi will soothe the pangs of hunger. Sometimes we get hungry because we don't eat. When we are hungry, we need to fill our stomach and make our body strong and healthy. In the same way, we often find that we are not able to accomplish the Dharma. We experience suffering. The afflictions arise and increase, and when that happens, we need to meditate. With the food of samadhi meditation, we can free ourselves from suffering by ridding ourselves of the afflictions.

◦ 49 ◦

Sip the best libation, the sweet nectar
Mindfulness, which flows without cessation, people of Dingri.

Will your body be properly cared for if you only eat food? No. Your mouth will get parched. When you are thirsty, you need to drink something. Then your thirst will be quenched and your body well cared for.

Similarly, when we meditate, sometimes we get overcome by distractions and we are not able to rest in equipoise within samadhi. Just as we need to drink if we get thirsty when we are eating, in our meditation we need the sweet libation of mindfulness and awareness. If we maintain our mindfulness and awareness when we meditate, we will not be distracted, and gradually we'll be able to attain the result.

These are instructions on how to practice samadhi with mindfulness and awareness. In the lineage of mahamudra that comes from Gampopa are instructions on the samadhi meditation of mahamudra. This is an excellent meditation, and the instructions have been taught by many great masters, including the various incarnations of the Karmapa. The Third Karmapa, Rangjung Dorje, taught them in his *Aspiration for Mahamudra*. The Ninth Karmapa, Wangchuk Dorje, taught them in *An Ocean of the Ultimate Meaning, Pointing Out the Dharmakaya,* and *Eliminating the Darkness of Ignorance*. These books show you the path that leads to liberation and omniscience. They contain wonderful instructions that you needn't doubt in any way. Read and study them. But don't study them as if they were just schoolbooks. Contemplate the teachings and then practice them. This will be extremely beneficial.

⋅ 50 ⋅

Trust the finest friend, awareness wisdom,
Who will never be apart from you, people of Dingri.

In the context of samadhi meditation, whether we are meditating on the nature of the mind or ascertaining the nature of the mind through logical inference, all phenomena have the aspect of emptiness, but they are not emptiness alone. There is also the aspect of clear wisdom. We need to nurture both the aspect of emptiness and the aspect of clear wisdom.

This clear awareness wisdom is like the companion of emptiness. It is what we call buddha nature—the seed of a buddha's wisdom, love, and power. The perfect wisdom of a buddha knows all phenomena as they are: the nature of all phenomena and all the varied appearances of phenomena. Buddhas also have great nonreferential compassion for all sentient beings.[5] And in addition to their great wisdom and great compassion, they also have the extraordinary power to engage in the activity of actually taking care of sentient beings. The seed of this is buddha nature. This buddha nature is the awareness wisdom, and we meditate upon this essence that is the union of clarity and emptiness. This essence is the friend who will never be apart from you.

⋆ 51 ⋆

Seek the finest child, the babe awareness,
Who is never born and never dies, people of Dingri.

Our awareness is like a child. As we take care of our child, he or she grows bigger and stronger. Similarly, at first our awareness is not all that clear, but it gradually gets clearer and stronger. As our meditation develops, the clear aspect, the pure aspect, and the stable aspect of our wisdom all gradually strengthen.

An actual child of flesh and blood is born and will eventually die. But the child that is awareness wisdom is unceasing activity that is not born and does not die. Therefore, if we just maintain this, it will continue to develop.

⋆ 52 ⋆

In the empty nature, whirl the lance of pure awareness.
There are no obstructions in the view, people of Dingri.

When we practice samadhi meditation, we need four things: the view, conduct, meditation, and result. These are taught in order. The first is the view.

All phenomena are empty by their nature, and they occur within emptiness. However, phenomena are not just emptiness; they are both emptiness and appearance, both emptiness and clarity. From a conventional perspective, this sounds like a contradiction: If something is empty, it cannot be clear awareness; and if something is clear awareness, it cannot be empty and void. If clarity is a thing and emptiness is nothing, they seem to be exclusive of each other. But this conventional understanding is not really how it is. Within emptiness, clear awareness can arise. And within clear awareness, there can also be emptiness.

When a martial artist whirls a lance around in a circle, the lance is not blocked by anything. It doesn't strike anything, and nothing stops it from twirling through space. In the same way, within emptiness you can also maintain clear awareness wisdom. Clear awareness wisdom is not obscured in any way by emptiness, and emptiness is not harmed in any way by clear awareness wisdom. Clarity and emptiness are not exclusive of each other; they are a unity. This is the proper view to hold. It is just as the great yogi Milarepa said in a song:

> Appearance, emptiness, and their indivisibility—
> These three are the view in brief.

External appearances and the empty essence of those appearances are not at all in conflict. Appearances do not conflict with emptiness. Emptiness does not conflict with appearances. The two are unified; they are indivisible. Milarepa's concise instructions in the song are the same as Padampa Sangye's instructions here.

This is the view of the union of appearance and emptiness. Conduct is next.

* 53 *

Train unceasingly in the spontaneous nature.
In conduct, there is nothing to give up or take up, people of Dingri.

Here conduct is said to be spontaneous. In terms of the view taught in the previous verse and the meditation taught next, we should not practice in a forced, blocked, or cramped way. The way to meditate is spontaneous. There is the empty aspect of the dharma expanse—you may also call it the clear aspect or buddha nature or wisdom—and from the first, its essence has been naturally present in the nature of the mind.

Because it is naturally present, there is no need to contrive to make it new or force it in your practice. The first point is to meditate within its natural arising.

Padampa Sangye says, "Train unceasingly." Within that natural spontaneity, like a river flowing downstream, naturally rest within samadhi. We should train unceasingly—not sometimes on and sometimes off.

In our conduct, there is nothing to block or give up, nor is there anything to adopt or take up. As it says in the earlier verse, "Grasp the finest object, your own constant nature." We meditate within the natural state. The natural state is not something we produce through meditation. When we are in samadhi meditation, sometimes we think, "I need my meditation to be really clear," or "I need my meditation to be really empty," or "I need the unity of clarity and emptiness." Thinking that we need to create something is what is called rainbow meditation. We do not need to meditate trying to create something like a rainbow. Just rest within the naturally present nature.

· 54 ·

In the thought-free nature, post the sentry nondistraction.
In meditation, there's no torpor or excitement, people of Dingri.

After establishing the view comes meditation. The view is recognizing the nature of the mind essence. Many people recognize the nature of mind and are able to maintain it, but sometimes they have the feeling that their recognition isn't progressing. Sometimes they think, "Maybe this is it," and sometimes they think, "Maybe it isn't." They have established the view but haven't been able to nurture it through meditation. You need to nurture the view in samadhi meditation.

When you meditate, should you try to either force the meditation in some way or block something from the meditation? No. Just relax and meditate. But this doesn't mean you should sit back and give free rein to all kinds of thoughts—greed, lust, anger, delusion, and so on—

without considering them a problem. That would be a sort of a laissez-faire meditation. That is not the way to relax.

Imbued with mindfulness and awareness, rest free of thought, including thoughts that cling to objects as real. As Padampa Sangye says, you need to post the sentry of mindfulness and awareness and rest without distraction. Nurture the meditation in this way and it will develop well, free of any torpor or excitement.

If you do not meditate properly, one of two problems may arise. One is torpor, a lack of clarity in meditation. The other is agitation or excitement, the arising of many thoughts. When you meditate without distraction, there is neither torpor nor excitement. If you can maintain such meditation, that is excellent. But sometimes you get lost in torpor or agitation, and you need to be able to eliminate them. The texts on mahamudra such as *Pointing Out the Dharmakaya* and *An Ocean of the Ultimate Meaning* contain many specific instructions on eliminating torpor and agitation by adjusting your posture and your conduct, by changing your motivation, and by applying remedies through meditation. These are extremely helpful.

The instruction here is simple and basic: just remain within nondistraction. In order to do this, you need to cultivate mindfulness and awareness so that you are not overcome by torpor or excitement. In terms of the view, there is not actually any torpor or agitation. They have never existed within the nature of the mind, and it is fine to meditate with confidence that they do not exist, which is what Padampa Sangye seems to be saying.

In a song, the yogi Milarepa said:

> Clarity, nonthought, and nondistraction—
> These three are the meditation in brief.

What should stable meditation be like? Meditation is not a state of complete blankness or nothingness. The mind's empty essence has the aspect of clarity, and the clarity of the mind is unceasing. Because of this clarity, thoughts often arise. Our meditation is naturally free of thoughts, and we need to rest undistracted within that through mind-fulness and awareness. Resting in such a way is what Padampa Sangye means by saying that our meditation is free from torpor and agitation.

· 55 ·

The inseparable four kayas are complete within your mind.
Do not fear or hope for the result, people of Dingri.

Following the view, conduct, and meditation, we come to the result. With the proper view, we can develop good conduct. Because of such conduct, we can cultivate correct meditation, and from our medita-tion, we can actually achieve the result. The ultimate result of Dharma practice is the excellent benefit for oneself and the excellent benefit for others.

We wish to free ourselves from suffering and to enjoy happiness. But this is not something that we do for ourselves alone. All other sentient beings want to be free from suffering and to be brought to the ultimate happiness. And the potential exists to bring about this ultimate benefit for others.

The ultimate result of the Dharma in general terms is what we call the perfect benefit for oneself and the perfect benefit for others. The perfect benefit for oneself is the attainment of the dharmakaya. What is the dharmakaya?

Our mind now has the fault of being full of confused thoughts, and we need to eliminate this faulty aspect. When we eliminate these thoughts, the qualities of perfect wisdom, perfect love, and perfect power can develop. The dharmakaya has all of these qualities of the Buddha. The meaning of the Tibetan word for Buddha, *sangye,* has two parts: "to purify" and "to develop." This is one way to understand the meaning of *buddha.* When you have eliminated and purified all the faults, the complete qualities naturally develop. This is attaining the result of the dharmakaya, which is the perfect benefit for oneself.

In terms of the perfect benefit for oneself, the clear, knowing wisdom aspect is called the dharmakaya, or body of qualities. The empty aspect is called the svabhavikakaya, or essence kaya. These two aspects together are the perfect benefit for oneself. Once we accomplish this perfect benefit for ourselves, how does this help others? We can help others because we have perfect wisdom, perfect love, and perfect power, the capability to help. With these qualities, the dharmakaya then emanates the form bodies, which are the perfect benefit for others.

Of these form bodies, the first is the sambhogakaya, or enjoyment body, which is visible to disciples who have pure karma. It is not something that ordinary individuals can see. Great bodhisattvas, those beings with pure karma, can see the sambhogakaya, which has what we call the five certainties of being born in the pure realm surrounded by all the bodhisattvas who have pure karma and are uninterruptedly turning the wheel of Dharma.[6] What is the sambhogakaya enjoying? It is enjoying the Dharma. This means that the sambhogakaya can teach all the different types of Dharma.

The sambhogakaya appears to beings who have pure perception. To all of us who have impure perception, what appears is the supreme nirmanakaya, or supreme emanation body. This form body appears in the impure realm, performs the twelve deeds, and in these ways accomplishes vast benefit for beings. The supreme nirmanakaya turns the wheel of Dharma, teaching the Dharma of the definitive meaning and of the provisional meaning, and brings many sentient beings onto the path to liberation.

These four bodies—the dharmakaya, svabhavikakaya, sambhogakaya, and nirmanakaya—are all perfect and complete within your mind right now. They are complete and inseparable within the buddha nature now. The buddha nature is present within the minds of all sentient beings, and so you can definitely attain the four kayas in the future. There is no need to have any hope or fear about this.

· 56 ·

The root of both samsara and nirvana
Comes down to mind—and mind has no reality, people of Dingri.

The view, conduct, meditation, and result have been explained, yet samsara may seem like a hard, solid thing that we have to eliminate. And nirvana may seem so far away. Can we actually get there? We definitely can eliminate samsara, and we can attain nirvana. The reason is this: samsara comes down to our mind, and the peace of nirvana also comes down to our mind. Samsara is not somewhere outside of our mind, and we don't have to travel a great distance to find a separate nirvana.

How does this verse help us? Since the mind is not a solid thing, we can eliminate what we need to eliminate and attain the results. The mind is not a real or concrete object. Understanding this does not require long explanations or logical proof. All you have to do is look, and you will see that there isn't a solid, truly established thing that is the mind.

Sometimes our thoughts seem big and coarse, but when we look at them, where are they? It's like the wind moving through space. When the wind blows, where is it? You can't find it anywhere. You can't say it's here; you can't say it's there. It's like our mind: the mind has no reality. And the root of both samsara and nirvana comes down to the mind.

· 57 ·

Lust and hate arise but leave no trace,
Like birds in flight; don't cling to passing moods, people of Dingri.

Even though the mind is the root of everything, our afflicted thoughts of greed, lust, and hatred appear, strong and powerful, and we engage in the greed and hatred. We think of something, and we think of it again and again, and it gets stronger and stronger. How do we get rid of these thoughts?

We experience the afflictions of desire and hatred, but their appearance is like the flight of a bird through the sky, leaving no tracks. They just dissolve into emptiness without leaving any trace. There is no reason to be attached or to fixate on them. They arise, and then they're the past, and they can't do anything to us.

Since everything comes down to the mind, we can attain the ultimate result. We are able to give up all of samsara because samsara is just the mind. We are able to achieve nirvana because nirvana is just the mind. The afflictions of desire and hatred sometimes seem like solid things that we can't get rid of. But if we look at their ultimate nature, how they actually are, we see that we can get rid of them. Since we have the instructions, we should have confidence that we can eliminate the afflictions of desire and hatred.

∗ 58 ∗

Unborn dharmakaya, like the essence of the sun,
Is a brilliant radiance that never ebbs or wanes, people of Dingri.

Often a self-deprecating, discouraged sort of laziness arises when we think about ourselves. We think that we are just ordinary sentient beings with afflictions and we can't possibly eliminate them. The result, the dharmakaya, seems so far away, so profound, that we think that there is no way we could ever achieve it. Actually, there is no need to think this way. We can attain the result because what is described in the treatises as the essence of the Buddha, buddha nature, is the seed of buddhahood present within all sentient beings. What is this essence? It is the unborn dharmakaya that is already present within our mind. Since it's unborn, it's not something that we need to create. All the qualities of the dharmakaya have been present within us from the very beginning.

Like the essence of the sun, the dharmakaya is brilliant radiance. When the sun is hidden by clouds, is its light any less brilliant, less strong, or less warm? No, it's unchanged; we just can't see it. When the clouds go away, we see the sun in all its brilliance, glory, and majesty. It's not that the sun hidden by the clouds has no such qualities and when the clouds go away, the sun suddenly develops these qualities. The sun has always been brilliant, glorious, and majestic. In the same way, the buddha nature present within us, the clear wisdom, is never diminished or less glorious. Since it is always present, we can make it manifest if we are diligent. If we remove the obscurations that temporarily veil it, then all the clarity, luminosity, and wisdom will come forth. There is absolutely no doubt that we can attain the ultimate result.

What obscures the buddha nature, the dharmakaya? Five faults obscure it: thoughts, feelings, hatred and desire, the movement of thoughts, and fixation. These are discussed in the following verses.

· 59 ·

Thoughts are like a burglar in an empty house.
There is really nothing there to gain or lose, people of Dingri.

The first of the five faults is thoughts. A continuum of various thoughts appears in our mind. These thoughts, however, are not fundamentally established as anything. Their essence is not anything at all. Thoughts occur, but they are empty by nature, so there is nothing that we can gain or lose from them.

It's like burglars in an empty house. Since there is nothing there for them to take, there is no reason to fear losing anything. There is a story from the life of the great yogi Milarepa. He was staying in a cave high in the mountains, and he had absolutely nothing in the cave. His only food was the nettles growing outside. One night some thieves came into his cave and looked everywhere for something to steal. Milarepa started laughing and said, "I can't find anything in the daytime. How are you going to find anything to steal at night?" If you don't have anything, there is nothing to fear losing. Since there is no substance to thoughts, they cannot be established as anything at all, so there is nothing at all to fear. You cannot lose or gain anything from thoughts.

◆ 60 ◆

Feelings leave no trace, like drawings sketched on water.
Do not cling to these confused appearances, people of Dingri.

Second among the five faults is feelings. Generally, in Buddhist philosophical texts, thought is presented as mind. In terms of the five aggregates, the primary aspect of mind is the aggregate of consciousness. This is taught as the six or eight consciousnesses. It is also called the primary mind, which is just mere awareness of an object.

Associated with consciousness are many different thoughts, which may be virtuous, unvirtuous, or neutral. Thoughts are mostly included in the aggregate of formations. There are many aspects to the aggregate of formations, but usually they are summarized as the fifty-one mental factors, which are basically coarse thoughts. If we look at these fifty-one mental factors, we find that one is coarser than the others. This is the factor of feeling. It is also presented as a separate aggregate itself, the aggregate of feeling, because we get attached to it and because feelings are so strong. When we have a good feeling, we get attached to it; when we have a bad feeling, we fear it. These feelings are coarse, strong thoughts that arise.

In order to eliminate our attachment to feelings, Padampa Sangye says that feelings are like drawings sketched on water that vanish without a trace. First we experience feelings, but then they disappear. When they disappear, like a drawing on water, they have no essence and are not anything at all. Because they disappear, they are confused appearances. We should not think that we need one feeling and do not need another. We do not need to fear them, cling to them, or fixate on them. Feelings just naturally disappear.

⋆ 61 ⋆

Thoughts of hatred and desire, like rainbows,
Cannot be identified or grasped, people of Dingri.

The third of the five faults is hatred and desire. Hatred and desire seem very strong, difficult, and harmful to us. We may feel that we have to try to get rid of them. We apply the remedies, but it is difficult to get rid of hatred and desire. However, if we realize that hatred and desire, in their very essence, are emptiness and are not established as anything, then they become like a rainbow in the sky.

When a rainbow appears in the sky, it looks brilliant and colorful, but because its essence is naturally empty, there is nothing there that could be an object to be attached to or feel aversion for. Similarly, there is no object to identify that is attachment or aversion.

In various meditation instruction manuals, this topic is often found in the sections called "taking the afflictions as the path." There are different ways to deal with the afflictions. One method is to suppress the afflictions; the main teachings of the Foundation Vehicle are about suppressing and preventing the afflictions. In contrast, the approach of the Mahayana and the secret mantra Vajrayana is to take the afflictions as the path. This does not mean that we somehow use the coarse afflictions. Rather it means that we develop good meditation and good recognition of the nature of the mind. Then, by looking at the essence of the afflictions, we are able to see that they are naturally empty and not established as anything at all.

Texts such as *Moonbeams of Mahamudra* and *Clarifying the Natural State* by Dakpo Tashi Namgyal contain instructions on taking the afflictions as the path and taking thoughts as the path. When you read these instructions, don't use them simply to develop an understanding of the view. You should not merely have the discernment that comes from study and is focused externally. If you look on the basis of meditational experience, you will be able to take afflictions as the path; if you have experience, the view, and realization, you will be able to take the afflictions as the path as described in the texts of Dakpo Tashi Namgyal.

But for the time being, the method to pacify the afflictions is to apply mindfulness, awareness, and carefulness to make sure that the afflictions don't arise. It is very important to be diligent about this.

• 62 •

Mental movements naturally dissolve
Like clouds in the sky; mind has no aim, people of Dingri.

Fourth is the movement or occurrence of thoughts. Generally, in samadhi meditation, first we learn tranquillity to develop stability of mind. When we are resting evenly within that stability, sometimes there is the movement of thoughts. Sometimes there are coarse, gross thoughts and sometimes a subtle undercurrent of thoughts. There are virtuous thoughts and unvirtuous thoughts. These are all the movement of the mind.

Mental movements naturally dissolve like clouds in the sky. If we are attached and cling to thoughts, will they dissolve by themselves? They will not. If we look at the essence of the movement, we see that it is empty by nature and cannot be established as anything at all. The movements of thoughts are not established anywhere inside the body or outside the body. Thoughts are naturally empty in essence. This is why they naturally dissolve. But they do occur, and when they occur they are like clouds in the sky. When clouds appear in the sky, they obscure the sun and moon, but they don't last forever. They naturally disperse. Similarly, the mind has no aim: there is no thought that we should do this or do that.

When we look at the movement of thought, this is what is known as looking at the mind in movement. The instructions on mahamudra in texts such as *Pointing Out the Dharmakaya, Eliminating the Darkness of Ignorance,* and *An Ocean of the Ultimate Meaning* describe looking at the mind in motion. First these instructions say to look at the resting mind, the mind in stillness. Then they say to look at the mind in motion. These profound instructions are extremely helpful to practice.

• 63 •

Nonfixation is self-liberated,
Like a breeze, with no clinging to objects, people of Dingri.

The last of the five faults is fixation. The other four—thoughts, feelings, desire and hatred, and the movement of the mind—should not be fixated upon. We should relate to them without any clinging or attachment. They are like the movement of wind. A light breeze blows for a while, and then it just stops. It doesn't harm anything. There is nothing to cling to, nothing to fixate on. It is the same with the movement of the mind, because thoughts are naturally empty.

The Vajradhara lineage prayer contains a verse about insight meditation that reads:

> The essence of thoughts is the dharmakaya, as is taught;
> Not anything at all yet arising as anything . . .

The essence of thoughts is the dharmakaya. Insight meditation means seeing the nature of everything. To explain this simply, we look at the essence of thoughts, and we see that by their nature, thoughts are naturally pure, the dharmakaya. The prayer continues:

> In an unceasing display. To this meditator,
> Grant your blessings that I realize the inseparability of samsara
> and nirvana.

Thoughts occur in an unceasing display. But as they arise, their essence is empty. There is no reason to cling to any object.

• 64 •

The previous few verses discussed things we need to eliminate—thoughts, feelings, attachment and aversion, and so forth. We are able to eliminate them because they are not established as anything by nature. For that reason, they are easy to give up. The next few verses discuss what we need to realize, why we can realize it, and the great qualities that arise from that realization. This is referred to as appearance and emptiness, awareness and emptiness, and bliss and emptiness by nature.

> Unfixated pure awareness is
> Like a rainbow in the sky above.
> Experience arises unimpeded, people of Dingri.

Pure awareness, the empty essence, the union of clarity and wisdom, the essence of the union of clarity and wisdom—these can all be called wisdom or awareness. This is the essence that is present within all sentient beings, yet we do not recognize it. We have the instructions to recognize it, and if we do, we should not fixate upon it. Pure awareness is without fixation. We should not cling to it or fixate on it in any way. It is like a rainbow in the sky above, and when we are without this fixation, experiences arise unimpeded, that is, without any blockages.

When we have this awareness, experiences can sometimes occur. We might experience bliss, clarity, or nonthought, but those don't really make any difference. The nature of awareness does not really change. If we nurture that and do not get attached to or fixated on experiences of bliss, clarity, or nonthought when they occur, they will not harm us as they will if we become proud of or attached to them. The method to prevent any harm is to have no fixation.

· 65 ·

> Realization of the dharma nature,
> Like a mute's dream, is beyond all words, people of Dingri.

When we realize the dharma nature, it's like the dream of a mute. A mute person may have a dream but cannot describe it. In the same way, when we experience the dharma nature, we cannot say it's like this or like that. We cannot describe it. The confused appearances of samsara can be described as having a shape, color, and so on. But the dharma nature cannot be described in any way. As it says in *The Way of the Bodhisattva*, "The ultimate is not the sphere of mind"—it is not the sphere of either mind or speech. For that reason, it is what Nagarjuna called "the inexpressible, inconceivable, and indescribable prajnaparamita." We cannot describe it in any way, but it is something we can experience. The great translator Marpa said in one of his songs, "Just like a mute tasting sugarcane, I have had an inexpressible experience." When we realize the dharma nature, we find that it is not something that we can describe in words.

• 66 •

Realization, like a young girl's joy,
Is an inexpressible delight, people of Dingri.

When we develop superior realization, we feel inexpressible delight in our mind. Normally, in samsara we experience fear and suffering because of our strong fixation on things. Fixating on things leads to clinging, and clinging results in all sorts of hopes and fears. First we develop hope, then fear that our hope will not be fulfilled. We are terrified of problems and difficulties. If we realize that the nature of all dharmas is empty, if we realize the empty nature of the mind, we are freed from those fears. That freedom is a delight that is inexpressible. Yet even though it transcends speech, we need words to point it out or represent it. So we use expressions such as the union of clarity and emptiness, the union of appearance and emptiness, the union of awareness and emptiness, and the union of bliss and emptiness. These terms are explained in the following verses.

⟡ 67 ⟡

Emptiness and clarity united,
Like the moon's reflection in the water,
Is not blocked or stuck on anything, people of Dingri.

Regarding the union of clarity and emptiness, clarity means the nature of the mind, which is emptiness. What is the nature of mind? There is nothing solid in the mind that we can find. There is no shape and no color to be found. The nature of the mind, the essence of the mind, is empty. But is this emptiness just blank, inanimate nothingness? No. It is clear in that it can know things; it is able to understand and be aware of things. This is what is meant by clarity. The essence of this clarity is empty, and the essence of emptiness is clarity. We can establish this through logic and inference, and by doing so we can develop certainty about the union of clarity and emptiness. We can also experience it in meditation. Through meditative experiences, we can come to know that the nature of the mind is this union of clarity and emptiness.

The analogy here is of the reflection of the moon in water. The reflection's essence is empty in that the moon is not actually in the water, yet it appears very clearly there. Nothing hides it or obscures it in any way. Therefore, there is nothing to be attached to and nothing that can be impeded. That is what the nature of the mind is like.

The union of clarity and emptiness, the union of appearance and emptiness, the union of awareness and emptiness, and the union of bliss and emptiness—what do these terms mean? Since emptiness means that nothing can be established by its nature, these terms are essentially the same, but they point out different aspects of emptiness. The union of clarity and emptiness means that the essence of the mind is emptiness and that emptiness has a clear aspect. It is able to know everything. The union of appearance and emptiness means that all appearances are mind and the mind is empty. All appearances are naturally empty, as is explained in the teachings of the Middle Way school. Regarding the union of awareness and emptiness, "awareness" in Tibetan is *rigpa,* which is a term used in the Dzogchen teachings. Rigpa is a particular synonym for the nature of the mind that indicates it is unlike any other experience. The union of bliss and emptiness means that the nature of the emptiness is exclusive of suffering of any kind. This nature cannot be established in any way, and there is nothing boring or problematic about that. By nature it is bliss; it is pleasurable.

⬧ 68 ⬧

Like the empty sky above, the mind,
Indivisible emptiness-appearance,
Has no center or periphery, people of Dingri.

This verse is about the indivisibility of appearances and emptiness. Various external appearances occur—visual forms, sounds, scents, tastes, and sensations—but their essence is naturally empty. Where do they occur? They occur in our mind. They appear in the nature of the mind. They seem to be external, but they cannot actually be established outside the mind in any way. All appearances are actually the mind.

There is what is called the reason of clear awareness, proof that everything is the mind. There are external appearances, and the reason there are is that they appear to the mind. There is no other thing that we can point to that does not appear to the mind. For that reason, appearances are mind. The nature of the mind is empty. Therefore appearances and emptiness are indivisible. Appearances occur, but while occurring, their essence is empty; while they are empty, they appear as anything. These two are inseparable. This inseparability is like the empty sky.

Appearances occur in the mind, and mind has no limits. You cannot say that the mind has a center or periphery that is either large or small. The nature of the mind is that it permeates everything—it has no center or periphery.

‧ 69 ‧

Thought-free nondistraction, like a beauty's mirror,
Has no limits and nothing to prove, people of Dingri.

A thought-free, undistracted mind is like a beautiful person's mirror. In a beauty's mirror, there is nothing to be proved or established, and there is no limit to what can appear. Padampa Sangye is saying that within the inseparability of appearance and emptiness we need to meditate without any thought or distraction.

‧ 70 ‧

Indivisible emptiness-awareness
Is like a reflection in a mirror.
It has no arising and no ceasing, people of Dingri.

Next is the inseparability of awareness and emptiness. The instructions on Dzogchen say that we should distinguish mind and awareness. How does one distinguish these two? Mind means the times when we do not see the essence—when we are distracted by many thoughts and our mind is moving. Because of that, we are unable to see how things truly are. Awareness means resting without distraction within the nature. The essence of awareness is empty, and that emptiness is clear. That is what we call awareness, or rigpa. Is the essence of the awareness something solid and truly existent? No, it is not. Awareness and emptiness are indivisible, and that indivisibility is like a reflection in a mirror. Reflections in a mirror cannot be established as anything, yet you see them. This is a simile for how awareness and emptiness appear.

Earlier, the image of the moon's reflection in water was used to represent the union of clarity and emptiness. Here, for the inseparability of awareness and emptiness, we have the reflection in a mirror. These have essentially the same meaning. Appearances occur, but their essence is empty. Clarity is clear, but its essence is empty. These are similes for the empty essence.

"It has no arising and no ceasing" means that awareness has been present from the very beginning. Though it has been present, it has been obscured by dualistic mind so we have not seen it. There is nothing in it that arises anew nor anything that ceases.

◆ 71 ◆

Emptiness inseparable from bliss
Is like the sunlight shining on the snow:
They cannot be differentiated, people of Dingri.

When we realize the nature of the mind, it is as was said in the earlier verse: "Realization, like a young girl's joy, is an inexpressible delight." The present verse is basically the same. The essence of bliss is empty, but it occurs with a blissful aspect. While it is empty, it is blissful; and while it is blissful, it is simultaneously empty. Bliss and emptiness are inseparable, like sunlight shining on snow. At the moment the light of the sun strikes the snow, it's brilliant and bright, but you cannot really distinguish the sunlight from the snow. You cannot say, "This is sunlight and that is snow." Similarly, you cannot divide bliss and emptiness, saying, "This is bliss and that is emptiness." The essence of the bliss is emptiness, and the essence of the emptiness is blissful. Like sunlight on snow, they are inseparable.

Up to this point, we have been primarily talking about the feelings and experiences that occur in meditative equipoise. Following this, Padampa Sangye addresses how we can maintain these feelings and experiences in postmeditation by relying on mindfulness and awareness.

· 72 ·

Deluded speech is traceless, like an echo.
There is nothing to cling to in sound, people of Dingri.

All sorts of appearances arise, and we have a lot of deluded conversations about them. Sometimes people say good things; sometimes people say bad things. Whether we hear good talk or bad talk, we need to engage it with mindfulness, awareness, and carefulness. If we do not apply mindfulness and awareness, then when someone says something nice to us, we might feel pride. Or a conversation may arouse jealousy, greed, or anger. When afflictions arise, they may cause us to accumulate negative karma, and this will end up harming us and others.

Actually, there is no need to follow these sounds. The sound of all talk is like the sound of an echo: you can hear it resound, but it has no essence whatsoever. There is no reason to grasp at it. If someone says something pleasant, there is no need to be attached to it. If someone says something unpleasant, there is no need to feel aversion or anger. Just rest within your meditation.

· 73 ·

Pain and pleasure's mechanism is
Like a lute's strings and its hollow body.
Your good circumstances come from actions, people of Dingri.

There is a cycle of pleasure and pain. Sometimes we experience happiness, and sometimes we experience suffering. These are like the sounding of a lute. Pleasure and pain occur because of actions. We might wish to create the happiness we want or block the pain we fear, but we cannot. The results of our actions will ripen, and when they do, what will help is our Dharma practice.

· 74 ·

Samsara and nirvana are self-liberated,
Like a child's game; the mind is free from aims, people of Dingri.

All kinds of confused appearances of samsara arise, and we want to free ourselves from samsara. But there is really nothing in these confused appearances to direct our mind toward. Appearances are naturally liberated. Their essence is empty.

It's like little children playing a game. Sometimes they do well at their game, and they get so excited and happy. Still, it is not of any actual benefit to them—it's just a game. And sometimes the game goes badly, and the children get so upset that they start crying. Actually there's no reason for the children to cry, since no one is harmed—it's just a game.

In other texts it is said, "Samsara is like a child's sand castle; there is no reason to be happy or upset about it." When children make a big, elaborate sand castle, they are happy and excited about it, and then when the tide comes in and washes it away, they get upset. But there is no reason at all to be excited about building a nice sand castle because it doesn't help anyone. And there is no reason to be upset when it's destroyed because this doesn't harm anyone. It does not have any significance.

It's the same way with ordinary beings and the confused appearances of samsara. We experience attachment and aversion toward these appearances, but there is nothing to actually focus on or aim at. So there is no need to have any hopes or fears about appearances. There is nothing in appearances to grasp on to.

· 75 ·

Outer fabrications are contained within the mind.
Solid ice will melt back into water, people of Dingri.

The things we see in the outer world can seem so brilliant, vivid, and compelling. Sometimes they are the objects of our desire, lust, and attachment. Sometimes they are the objects of our hatred and aversion.

Many things can become the objects of our attachment or aversion, and what do they all come down to? They are not ultimately external things. The root of everything is our internal mind.

Water frozen into ice is hard, solid, and difficult to break. But since it is essentially just water, it melts into liquid. In the same way, if we do not experience greed and aversion toward external things, and if we practice the Dharma and rest in the equipoise of natural samadhi, we cannot be harmed by objects that create greed, aversion, and delusion. As it says, "Solid ice will melt back into water."

* 76 *

Ignorance's mechanism works
Like the welling of a meadow spring.
Blocking it won't stop its flowing forth, people of Dingri.

The root of the confused appearances of samsara is ignorance. We generally think of ignorance as the first of the twelve links of interdependence—not knowing about karma, cause, and effect. In the practice of mahamudra, it is taught that the root of samsara is not recognizing the nature of the ordinary mind.

The great early master of the Kagyu lineage Pakmo Drukpa went to many lamas and asked them, "What is the root of the confused appearances of samsara? What causes samsara?" First he went to the great Kadampa master Chökyi Senge, who replied, "The root of samsara is the ignorance that is the first of the twelve links of interdependence." Pakmo Drukpa said, "I don't understand. I'm not sure what that means." He had a lot of doubt.

He went to the Sakya master Kunga Nyingpo and asked him, "Master, what is the root of samsara?" Kunga Nyingpo said, "The root of samsara is the winds from the right and left channels not entering the central channel." Pakmo Drukpa responded, "What does that mean? I don't understand." Again he had a lot of doubt.

Then he went to Gampopa and asked, "Please, Master, tell me, what

is the root of samsara?" Gampopa said, "The root of samsara is not recognizing the ordinary mind." And Pakmo Drukpa said, "Ah! I understand! We have to recognize this ordinary mind, and if we do, there are
instructions that can free us from samsara." He developed great faith
and belief in this, and he became Gampopa's disciple and one of the
main figures of the four elder and eight younger Kagyu lineages.

This ignorance that does not recognize the ordinary mind is like the
mechanism of samsara. What is the antidote for this? It is to rest in meditation within the nature of our mind. We cannot stop this ignorance. If
we tried to stop this ignorance, it would be like trying to stop the water
flowing from a spring in a meadow. When water gushes forth from a
spring, if you try to block it on the right, it will flow to the left. If you
try to block it on the left, it flows to the right. If you try to plug it, it will
burst the plug out. You cannot stop it.

· 77 ·

The delusions of samsara and nirvana
Are just like encounters with an enemy.
Practice virtue as your friend and ally, people of Dingri.

The deluded appearances of samsara sometimes appear as friends and
sometimes as enemies, like robbers or thieves. These appearances can
be very powerful, so there's a danger that we could lose our life or all our
money or possessions when we encounter them. We need an ally—a
friend or champion—to help us so that we don't have difficulties when
we meet enemies. Who is that ally? Our ally is the practice of virtue.
If we practice virtue with our body, speech, and mind, we can actually
accomplish virtue, and this will help protect us from enemies—all
the confused experiences of samsara—so that they will not be able to
harm us.

Among the different virtues that we can practice, the supreme is the
practice of bodhichitta. As the great bodhisattva Shantideva said in the
first chapter of *The Way of the Bodhisattva*:

Just as you follow a hero when in danger,
Why would the careful not rely upon
That which will free you instantly when relied on?

The great hero is bodhichitta. When we go to a terrifying place, there
is the danger that we will lose our life or possessions. Padampa Sangye
says that we need to practice virtue, and the best virtue is bodhichitta.
If we develop bodhichitta, we will be able to free ourselves from danger
easily. As Shantideva said, why would you not rely upon such a hero for
protection? In other words, we should rely upon bodhichitta.

To generate bodhichitta, we can recite a long prayer or a short one,
or we can just make a brief aspiration. There are many texts for going
for refuge and developing bodhichitta, and whichever one we recite,
developing bodhichitta brings immeasurable virtue, which will free us
from fear and suffering.

As said above, the various confused appearances of samsara and nirvana arise like encounters with enemies. When we have done great misdeeds, the danger is that the result will ripen on us. We want to make
sure that we don't experience the results of the grave misdeeds we've
done. We don't want to fear such suffering in this life or in future lives.

It is said that even if we have committed a terrible act that would ripen
as rebirth in the hells, by developing bodhichitta we might be reborn in
a hell realm for an instant and then immediately be freed. Or we may
have karma that would lead to rebirth in the hells, but if we develop
bodhichitta, we might only get a headache and through the headache
purify that karma. In this way, we can purify our misdeeds by developing bodhichitta. That is the meaning of practicing virtue as our ally.

⋅ 78 ⋅

The natural clarity of the five kayas
Is spread before you like a land of gold.
Do not hope or fear, reject or take up, people of Dingri.

The ultimate result of the practice, the five kayas, is present within us, and it is compared to a land of gold. The result of the five kayas is right here, ready and waiting for us to achieve it. There's no need to have any hope or fear about anything. We only need to rest in the nature of the mind. There is nothing in particular that we need to take up or give up.

⋅ 79 ⋅

Precious human life's a treasure island.
Don't come back an empty-handed fool, people of Dingri.

We have attained a precious human body with all the freedoms and riches, and this is uniquely fortunate. The precious human body is often compared to a treasure island. When you go to an island of treasure, what do you do? You carry away as much treasure as you can.

This metaphor comes from India during the time of the Buddha. At that time, India was a vast, spacious, and extremely wealthy country. Even though it now seems rather poor and underdeveloped, at that time it was developed and prosperous. The country prospered because merchants sailed to treasure islands that surrounded India, where there were jewels of many kinds. They would sail to these islands, fill their boats with as many jewels as they could carry, and return to India.

But doing this was not easy. Their ships were small and not the best of ships. Since they were sailing across the ocean, sometimes they would be impeded by rough seas. Or they might encounter a sea monster or a whale that would wreck their ship. Going to the treasure islands took a lot of courage. The merchants who took this journey had to disregard all their fears and all the dangers to their life. When they got to the treasure islands, all they needed to do was to carry off as many jewels as they could.

What if one of the merchants were to rouse the courage to get on the ship and endure the ordeal of the journey, disregard all the dangers to his life and limb, ignore all his fears, finally arrive at this treasure island, and then decide not to bother taking any jewels and just go back empty-handed? What kind of fool would do that?

It's the same for us now that we have this precious human life. Because we have this human life, we can obtain Dharma instruction and practice, and by doing this, we can help ourselves and others. This is truly the cause for bringing ourselves and others great happiness. Now that we have this opportunity, we have to practice the Dharma. We have to accomplish something for ourselves and others. Otherwise, if we just let it go to waste, this human life is pointless. It doesn't help us in any way. Don't come back an empty-handed fool. Now that we have this precious human body, we need to use it for practice.

◆ 80 ◆

Mahayana Dharma is a wish-fulfilling jewel.
Search long as you may, it will be hard to find again, people of Dingri.

Among the different types of Dharma, such as the Dharma of the Foundation Vehicle and the Mahayana, what we practice is generally the Dharma of the Mahayana.

Performing pujas, ritual recitations, smoke offerings, and so on are all extremely helpful. In the short term, these practices help dispel obstacles to Dharma practice as well as other kinds of difficulties in life. They are also causes for attaining the ultimate result. If we can thus practice the Dharma in stages, this is wonderful.

We also have the companionship of the sangha. As it is said, "The unsurpassable guide is the precious sangha." The sangha is our companions, and we can help one another. When we are not feeling diligent, our companions can help us feel more diligent. When we don't feel much interest or faith, our companions can help us feel more interest and faith. When we aren't quite able to practice, they can encourage us in our practice. In this way, the companionship of the sangha is a great help to us as we practice the Dharma.

All of this is like a wish-fulfilling jewel, which is something that, search long as you may, will be hard to find again. You cannot be sure that you will be able to find the Dharma of the Mahayana ever again. Now that you have this wish-fulfilling jewel right in your hands, this is the time to put it to use diligently. Being able to do so is extremely fortunate.

◆ 81 ◆

Come what may, in this life you'll have clothes and food enough.
Concentrate on what is most important—Dharma practice,
people of Dingri.

Even if you don't necessarily do great things in this life, when it comes to food, clothing, possessions, and wealth, whatever happens, things will work out somehow. The essence of what you really need is to concentrate on what is most important. If you think that everything you need to do in this life is important and you can put off the Dharma, this will be a terrible loss for you in the future. If instead you lose out a little in this life and devote yourself entirely to Dharma practice, this will help you greatly in the future. You need to be diligent about Dharma practice and put everything you have into it.

◆ 82 ◆

Take on hardships while you are still young.
When you're old, your body won't endure it, people of Dingri.

Dharma practice sometimes involves hardships and difficulties, and you need to be able to withstand them. For example, among the special preliminary practices, you have to do one hundred thousand prostrations. Is it difficult? Yes, but you have to be diligent about it nonetheless. You need to do this when you are young, because that's when you can put the effort into it. If while you are young, you get distracted by all kinds of worldly pleasures and pains and don't practice, later when you are old and bent, it will be much harder. If you want to do one hundred thousand prostrations, you won't be able to. Therefore, you need to do these prostrations now while you are young and healthy. When you are old, your body won't endure it.

◆ 83 ◆

When afflictions come, apply the antidote.
Concepts will be naturally freed, people of Dingri.

Sometimes afflictions arise. Do they arise because we are poor, miserable, and unfortunate? No, they arise because we have imprints of the afflictions from beginningless time. When the afflictions occur, we address this in Dharma practice by suppressing them with an antidote. For example, if hatred arises, we apply an antidote and meditate on patience.

Sometimes we think, "I want to get rid of these afflictions, but I just can't do it." But that is not the way it is, because actually the afflictions are fleeting; they are adventitious. They are like clouds that hide the sun. The light of the sun is always naturally present. Clouds are just temporary; eventually the wind will come along and blow them away. In the same way, the nature of the mind is naturally present, and the obscurations and the afflictions are just adventitious. When we use an antidote against the afflictions, sometimes we will be able to suppress the afflictions, but sometimes we won't. Even though we sometimes can't, if we gradually keep trying, eventually we accustom ourselves to doing it. Because the afflictions are not present in the real nature, we can suppress and decrease them. They are not established as anything, and therefore we can eliminate them. They will just naturally disappear.

+ 84 +

Now and then recall samsara's faults.
This will serve to clarify your faith, people of Dingri.

In this samsaric world, we sometimes encounter difficulties, problems, and obstacles. When this happens, we should not think, "Oh, I'm so unfortunate. Everything goes badly for me." The fact is that suffering does occur in samsara. Problems and difficulties occur, and when they happen to us, we need to realize it is not just a temporary situation—it is a characteristic of samsara. This is what samsara is like.

As it is said, "The end of birth is dying; the end of meeting is parting; the end of building is falling; the end of gathering is using up." We can build a house, but no matter how large it is, eventually it will collapse and become ruins. Think about the huge structures that were built in earlier epochs, buildings that were made with great difficulty out of enormous stones, and yet in the end, they all just collapsed into ruins.

We can read in history books about the great people of the past who were amazingly skillful, powerful, scholarly—they were great heroes and wonderful people. But they lived hundreds or thousands of years ago. Is that hero from hundreds or thousands of years ago still here? That is all in the past. There is nothing left of it. This is just the way this samsaric world is. It is by nature suffering. When unfortunate circumstances happen to us, can we help ourselves? Yes, we can, but not by looking for a short-term solution to remove our problems temporarily. Rather, we need to try to free ourselves from samsara entirely.

We do this by practicing the Dharma: by praying to the Three Jewels, going for refuge, and developing bodhichitta. By doing this, we not only free ourselves from the suffering of samsara, but we can also bring great benefit to many sentient beings from now until samsara is entirely emptied. This comes about because of the Dharma. Recalling this will serve to clarify our faith. This is why it is so helpful to think about the defects of samsara.

· 85 ·

Now be diligent and hold that ground.
This will guide you on the path at death, people of Dingri.

We are extremely fortunate to have gained the wonderful support of a human body in this life. We have been able to enter the gate of the Dharma, and we have this opportunity to practice. All this is truly great fortune. However, there is always a slight danger that we might lose ourselves to laziness. It is important not to be overcome by laziness but to be diligent about practicing.

We need to hold our ground and actually help ourselves. How is it helpful to practice the Dharma? It will guide us along the path at death. If we do not take this opportunity to practice the Dharma now, in the future we might take a good birth or a bad birth—it's not at all certain. Therefore, it's important to practice the Dharma wholeheartedly. Then we can say to ourselves, "I really practiced the Dharma," and when we pass away, this will guide us along the path. This is why it is so important to practice with great joy and delight.

· 86 ·

If you don't have time now, then when will you?
You get fed but one time in a hundred, people of Dingri.

We have been in samsara since beginningless time, and we would remain here endlessly, except that now we have this wonderful opportunity to do something to truly benefit ourselves and to attain a great result. This comes from having a precious human body with its eighteen leisures and riches. To have this human body, enter the gate of the Dharma, and start practicing the Dharma is extremely good fortune. In fact, it is extraordinary.

One hundred years ago, there was no opportunity to practice the Dharma in the West. Buddhism first spread in India, and Western countries are separated from India by vast oceans. Until recent times, the Dharma had not spread to this part of the world: it was simply too far away. Now it seems that the amazing compassion and activity of the Buddha is pushing the Dharma beyond India, and the amazing faith and devotion of Western disciples is pulling it to the West. Not everyone has the opportunity to encounter the Dharma. But the compassion of the Buddha and the faith of Western students have come together to create this exceptional opportunity that is just one time in a hundred.

We have this extremely fortunate opportunity to practice the Dharma now, but often we think, "I really want to practice the Dharma today, but I have a lot of things to do. There's no time today. I'll practice the Dharma tomorrow." But then tomorrow something else comes up, and we put it off for days or weeks or months. There is always something else we need to do. If we are not free to practice the Dharma now, when will we ever be free? We have to decide that the Dharma is what is important. We need to make the time to practice the Dharma. If we do not have time today, we are not going to have time tomorrow or next month or next year—then when will we ever have time to practice the Dharma? Now we have this opportunity, so we need to use it and really practice the Dharma. This is extremely important.

· 87 ·

Life's uncertain—fleeting as the dew on grass.
Don't be lazy, don't be indolent, people of Dingri.

Now is the time when we need to put aside the little things and do the important things. This is our chance: we have this wonderful human body, and we have encountered the Dharma. We need to practice the Dharma now, because we cannot be certain when we will have the chance again. We cannot even count on remaining alive.

Life is uncertain, as brief as dew on grass. Dewdrops on a blade of grass don't last long at all. As soon as the sun strikes them, they dry up and disappear. In the same way, our human life does not last long. It is impermanent by nature. Particularly now, in developed countries, there are many ways we can die. We could die in a car or train accident or a plane crash. Not only that, these days there are many people who have mistaken ideas and evil intentions and they commit acts of terrorism. We never know whether we'll be killed by a terrorist. Many things can bring our death at any time; it's not at all certain how long we will live. Now that we have this opportunity to practice the Dharma, we need to be diligent about it.

If we practice the Dharma, then at least we can have some mental ease should something untoward happen to us. When a fearsome situation occurs, the Dharma will help. Also, we will be able to say, "At least I did as much Dharma practice as I could." If we have first-rate diligence, that is best. But even if we do only a little bit of Dharma practice, we can still have a real sense of confidence in our mind and think, "I did some Dharma practice, and that is going to help." This is why we need to make sure that we don't let ourselves be overcome by sloth and laziness. We need to put aside distractions and engage in practice as much as we can.

· 88 ·

If you were to slip and fall from here,
Finding human birth again would not be easy, people of Dingri.

Now we are on the excellent path of the Dharma, but it is a narrow path, so we have to be careful. If we slip and fall from it, it will be difficult to get up and find a human birth again. It is difficult to gain a human life without encountering the Dharma. If we can accomplish the Dharma, it will not be so difficult to attain a human life again.

The previous verse says that life is uncertain, and many fearsome circumstances can occur, but we have in our hands the methods that can help us at such times. If we practice the Dharma, we have something to do when we encounter terrifying situations. When we leave this human life, can we attain a human life again? Generally, it is very difficult to attain a human life, but we have the method to do so, the true Dharma, and if we practice it now, we will be able to attain a human life again. But if we let this human life go to waste, we will not be able to achieve one in the future. This is why it is so important not to let this life go to waste.

· 89 ·

Like the sunlight breaking through the clouds,
The Buddha's teachings are here just for now, people of Dingri.

There are times when the Buddha's teachings spread, and this is because of the special activity of the Buddha and the fortunes of his students. There are also times when the teachings weaken and disappear. It's like the sunlight breaking through the clouds. On a cloudy day, the sun may break through the clouds for a moment, but then another cloud passes over and the sun disappears.

The Buddha's teachings are here just for now. This is the moment when the sun is shining through the clouds. Now we have attained a precious human body, and the Buddha's teachings have spread; these things have come together for just this one moment. That is why this opportunity to encounter the Dharma is incredibly fortunate and it is so important that we do not let this opportunity go to waste.

When the Buddha appeared in India in ancient times, he turned the wheel of Dharma and the Dharma spread. In the great monastic universities of India such as Nalanda and Vikramashila, Buddhism shone like the sun. An inconceivable number of great masters appeared: great teachers, great masters of meditation, and great scholars. If you go to India now, it's quite possible that you would encounter the Dharma, but it's also possible that you will go places where you won't find any Dharma. The place that was the hub of the Buddhist teachings in India is now the state of Bihar, and if you go there now, all you will see are just the traces of where Buddhism flourished at places like Nalanda. You could take a tour of these ruins and think, "A great monastery used to be here, but nothing is happening here now," but that doesn't really help you. But if you look at these ruins and feel faith, thinking, "This is the place where great masters taught and Buddhism flourished. Now I have the opportunity to practice the Dharma," this encourages you to have faith and devotion and is very helpful. But simply to look at the stones at a historical site is of no benefit at all.

There are times when the Buddhist teachings spread and times when they decline and disappear. Now is a time when the Buddha's teachings have spread—the sun is shining through a break in the clouds. The Buddha's teachings are here just for now. We have encountered the Dharma, entered the gate of the Dharma, and developed confidence and courage that we can practice it. Now that we have this chance, if we practice the Dharma 100 percent, that is really wonderful. Even if we only do a little study and practice and generate a bit of faith and belief, it is extraordinarily fortunate to have this opportunity.

⋅ 90 ⋅

You talk cleverly but do not practice.
You're the ones concealing hidden faults, people of Dingri.

It is extremely fortunate to study the Dharma and learn about it. However, there is the danger that we might learn a little bit about the Dharma and then think that we can explain it well to other people, even though we don't actually practice it ourselves. This is a problem. If we have this fault, we need to know it. We are the ones concealing hidden faults.

These days in developed countries, many people are writing books and publishing magazines about the Dharma, and this is wonderful. But sometimes these books criticize Buddhism. Sometimes they say things like, "In the biographies of the masters from the past, there are some stories that couldn't have actually happened. These are superstitious beliefs. They're not really true or real." On one hand, it doesn't make a difference if there are books or magazines like this, but on the other hand, we need to remember that the unsurpassable guide is the precious sangha. Our sangha or community guides people into the Dharma, so if instead of bringing people into the Dharma, we separate people from the Dharma, this is a problem. When we write books and magazine articles, we need to do it in order to help sentient beings. It can help other sentient beings and bring us great merit as well. If we help other people enter the Dharma, then this is a really vast kind of help. We need to understand this properly.

If we say that there are faults in the Dharma, that it's superstitious and not really true, people may not understand. It's not their fault; it's because of their habitual tendencies from beginningless time, so they might not know. Then there is the danger that they will think that the Dharma is mistaken and false and develop misconceptions and wrong views about the Dharma. It's good to have a lot of books about the Dharma, but when we write books and magazine articles, it's important to do this out of a wish to help, with a kind heart, and in a way that helps people develop faith and belief in the Dharma.

I think that if I were to meet Padampa Sangye, I would have to say, "I'm sorry, Padampa Sangye. Don't scold me. I realize this is my problem. I know a lot about the Dharma, but I don't really practice." It's important that we don't just mouth the Dharma that we have learned but actually put it into practice. If we are not able to do that, it is a real fault. We should never let this problem of knowing about the Dharma but never actually putting it into practice occur.

◆ 91 ◆

Faith is easily swayed by circumstances.
Contemplate the defects of samsara, people of Dingri.

Sometimes when we encounter favorable circumstances, our faith in the Dharma increases, and when we encounter difficulties and bad circumstances, our faith diminishes. We need a way to make sure that our faith grows and does not diminish. What is the method? We need to think about the defects of samsara.

From time to time we encounter pain and suffering, obstacles, and difficulties. When these occur, we need to realize that this is not anyone's fault; it is just the nature of samsara. What we need is a method to free ourselves from samsara, and that method is the Dharma. If we understand this, our faith will not diminish but will grow. We need to contemplate samsara's faults.

◆ 92 ◆

Bad friends naturally lead to bad behavior.
Look to your own mind for making judgments, people of Dingri.

A good friend is someone who encourages you toward the Dharma, a spiritual friend. Bad friends are those who separate you or draw you away from the Dharma, saying that the Dharma is no good. Therefore you should look to your own mind for making judgments. Think carefully about what is good and what is bad. Consider this well and think about what you need to do to progress in the future.

· 93 ·

Ignorant confusion is the demon source of ruin.
Hold fast to awareness and mindfulness, people of Dingri.

The afflictions are known as the three poisons or the five poisons. Why are they called poisons? A poison is something that harms us—it might take our life or make us ill if we eat or drink it. The three or five poisons are only thoughts. Thoughts might be good or bad; the poisons are harmful thoughts that can bring us suffering and create obstacles and difficulties. This is why the Buddha called them the poisons: to let us know that we need to eliminate them. But whether we talk about three poisons or five poisons, the main poison is ignorance. Ignorance is not knowing what we should take up and what we should give up.

As Gampopa told the great master Pakmo Drukpa, the root of samsara is the ignorance of not recognizing the ordinary mind. This is the confusion that is ignorance, and because of it we commit all sorts of bad actions, accumulate negative karma, experience many problems, and bring ourselves more and more suffering. The root of all of this, the demon source of ruin, is the ignorance of not knowing our ordinary mind.

We need to eliminate this ignorance of not recognizing the ordinary mind, and the way to do this is through meditation. In meditation, we need awareness and mindfulness. We need to look at the nature of the mind and rest in meditation. The main method of practice is to follow the instructions on mahamudra, but it is very rare for someone to simply sit down, practice mahamudra, and suddenly recognize the ordinary mind. This is why the great masters taught that first we have to do the creation-phase visualizations of deities and then the completion-phase practices. Before doing these, we need to do the preliminary practices:

the common preliminaries of contemplating the four thoughts that turn the mind to the Dharma and the special preliminaries of prostrations and so forth. We practice these in order, without becoming distracted, always maintaining mindfulness and awareness. As we sit in meditation with the body, we need mindfulness and awareness in our mind, or the meditation does not help us. As we do the physical practices of the preliminaries such as prostrations or mandala offerings, we also need to maintain mindfulness and awareness in our mind. Through this we can develop our faith and devotion. When we do virtuous things with our body and our speech, we need to have mindfulness and awareness in our mind at the same time.

· 94 ·

Don't cling to the poisons and the path is short.
Generate strong antidotes against them, people of Dingri.

Because of ignorance, the five poisons of greed, hatred, delusion, pride, and jealousy arise. Because of these five poisonous afflictions, we harm ourselves and we harm others. Among these five poisons, the most harmful are the three poisons of greed, hatred, and delusion. We need a way to eliminate these poisons, an antidote against them. The antidote for the afflictions is not to cling to them. This is a strong antidote, which is what we need. Applying a weak antidote against the strong affliction of ignorance will not help us much. We need to be careful to rely on the antidote, which is not to fixate on or cling to the afflictions.

· 95 ·

If your diligence is weak, you're lost.
Don the armor so that you will get there, people of Dingri.

We need to rely on antidotes for the five or three poisons, and in particular for ignorance, which is the chief among them. In order to apply the antidotes, we need diligence. Eliminating the afflictions and increasing our virtue does not happen without effort. This is because we have been accustomed from beginningless time to all the confused appearances of samsara. We have strong imprints of this in our mind, and because of these imprints, ignorance and the other afflictions arise again and again. The afflictions are only adventitious, fleeting stains, and so they can be eliminated, but they are difficult to eliminate. Because the afflictions are the root of suffering, we need to make sure that we eliminate them, and in order to do so, we need to rouse as much diligence as we can.

Generally, the afflictions are strong and the antidotes are weak. It's as if the antidotes and the afflictions are at war. We need to make sure that the antidotes are well armed, and then we can eliminate the afflictions. This means we need strong diligence. Without diligence, the antidotes will not have any power against big fears and afflictions. We need armor-like diligence, which is courageous, strong, powerful diligence. There are two types of diligence: continual diligence and this armor-like diligence. Continual diligence is extremely important, but sometimes we need real strength and real courage to eliminate the afflictions that are difficult to overcome. At that point, we need to don the armor of this strong diligence.

· 96 ·

Mind's propensities are like old friends
Who keep on coming back; don't chase the past, people of Dingri.

Sometimes we can be extremely diligent about subduing ignorance and the afflictions, but sometimes they keep coming back and we cannot be diligent. We have become accustomed to these bad propensities since beginningless samsara, and so sometimes we can only partially eliminate them. We want to develop the qualities of realization, and sometimes they come, but sometimes they don't. This is just how things are. Our habitual tendencies are old acquaintances; we go way back with them. We need to try to get rid of our old bad habits and create new good habits. When we create good habits, sometimes they take hold and sometimes they don't. We need to be continually diligent about this. Our old habits are harmful. Don't chase the past.

· 97 ·

If your understanding and realization
Are deficient, supplicate your master.
Samadhi will be born within your mind, people of Dingri.

Sometimes when we listen to the Dharma, it can be difficult to develop our understanding. And sometimes when we meditate, it can be difficult to develop experience and realization. How can we develop our understanding and our realization? Padampa Sangye says, "Supplicate your master, and samadhi will be born within your mind." If we supplicate our root and lineage lamas, it will help, because deep meditation will be born in us.

As it is said in the Vajradhara lineage prayer, "Devotion is the head of meditation." If we have faith and devotion, what will happen? "As ones who continually supplicate the lama who opens the gate to the treasury of oral instructions, please bless us that genuine devotion is born in us." We need to supplicate the lama and to be diligent about guru yoga practice, because through this we will develop real samadhi, real meditation within ourselves.

This metaphor of devotion as the head of meditation is a wonderful metaphor. If we think about our body, we have a little head and a big body. Which one is more important? At first it might seem that our big body must be more important than our little head. Actually, if we were to lose an arm or a leg, it would be difficult, but we could manage. There are even people who have no arms or legs but are able to lead good lives because they have a good head. But if we cut off our head, we couldn't do anything at all. Devotion is like the head of our meditation.

If you have good devotion, then samadhi will be born in you. Supplicate your master and deep meditation will be born in you. In particular, we need to make efforts at guru yoga practice.

· 98 ·

If you wish for future happiness,
Tolerate the hardships of the present.
Buddhahood is right here next to you, people of Dingri.

The future and the present might seem more or less the same, but the future lasts much longer—a very long time. We need to be happy in the future. If we want to gain happiness, we need to tolerate the hardships of the present. We need to exert ourselves to practice the Dharma with diligence, and the basis for achieving happiness, buddhahood, is right next to us and not difficult to find. For that reason it is good to practice diligently.

· 99 ·

This old yogi cannot stay in Dingri—
I'm off. Cut through misconceptions now, people of Dingri.

"This old yogi" refers to the word *atsara,* a Tibetan term for an ordinary Indian practitioner. This is a nickname that Padampa Sangye received because of an event in his life, although the lives of masters such as Padampa Sangye can really be understood only by great meditators.

At the beginning of his life, Padampa Sangye was actually known as the great scholar Kamalashila, who was extremely beautiful and handsome. One day he went to a village where the corpse of a person who had died of a horrendous illness lay in the middle of the road. Everyone was afraid that this terrible disease would spread throughout their village, so no one would touch the corpse, and they couldn't move it.

Kamalashila had a particular instruction for ejecting his consciousness from his body and then inhabiting another body. Out of unbearable compassion for the people of the village, he used this instruction. He ejected his consciousness, entered the corpse, and animated it, and then he just walked away in the corpse to a place far away where no one would go and everything would be fine.

While he was doing this, along came another meditator who had the same instructions. But this other meditator was quite ugly. When he came along and saw Kamalashila's handsome, fresh corpse, he thought, "This is my chance!" So he ejected his consciousness into Kamalashila's corpse and walked away in this new, beautiful body. When Kamalashila had disposed of the corpse, he left it and returned with just his mind. But all that remained was this ugly corpse of the other mahasiddha. What could he do? He had no choice but to enter this other meditator's corpse.

Padampa Sangye and Kamalashila have different bodies, but in essence the same mind. Later Padampa Sangye went to Tibet and to China and he helped spread the Dharma. He spent the end of his life in Dingri and gave these instructions there. He told the people of Dingri, "This is the end of my life. Cut through your misconceptions now."

+ 100 +

I myself am always undistracted.
Follow my example, people of Dingri.

Finally Padampa Sangye says, "I myself am always undistracted in my mind, and through practicing in this way I have attained great accomplishment. You too should do the same. If you practice without distraction, if you engage in the Dharma, this is the kindest thing you can do for yourself. You should also follow my example."

* * *

In his *One Hundred Verses of Advice,* Padampa Sangye gives instructions on how to devote our entire lives to Dharma practice, addressing the worldly aspects of our lives—how to relate to our families and our work—as well as our Dharma practice itself. He primarily focuses on the preliminaries: the four thoughts that turn the mind, the need to develop bodhichitta, and the importance of having a good heart. Recalling Padampa Sangye's words and contemplating their meaning will help us develop a pure and wholehearted motivation, so these instructions are beneficial and necessary for us no matter what our level, whether we have just entered the gate of the Dharma or whether we have been meditating for a long time. They will help us both in the short term of this life as well as in the long term of progressing through the stages of our Dharma practice. For this reason, I encourage you to please take them to heart and practice them as much as you can.

NOTES

✦ ✦ ✦

1. There are many different versions of *One Hundred Verses of Advice for the People of Dingri*. The one used here is from *The Treasury of Precious Instructions* compiled by the great teacher Jamgön Kongtrul Lodrö Thaye, which collects all the Dharma instructions of the Eight Chariots of the Practice Lineages that spread in Tibet, one of which is the lineage of the pacification of suffering that was taught by Padampa Sangye and many other masters. Of course, all Dharma is about the pacification of suffering, but Padampa Sangye's lineage is a particular distillation of the instructions from the teachings on transcendent wisdom, or prajnaparamita, and so it is called the pacification of suffering that is the distillation of the prajnaparamita. The teachings from this lineage are contained in one of the volumes of *The Treasury of Precious Instructions,* and this text of *One Hundred Verses of Advice for the People of Dingri* is found there, where it is called the *Eighty Verses of Advice*. Other than a few minor differences in wording, there is no difference in the actual instructions; it is only a different enumeration and a different name.

2. This sentence refers to the Four Dharmas of Gampopa, a short teaching that encapsulates the essence of the Kagyu practice. Your mind going toward the Dharma means that your mind turns away from the temporary pleasures of this life. The Dharma becoming the path means that you develop revulsion for samsara and become intent on liberation. The path dispelling confusion means that motivated by bodhichitta, you train in the Mahayana path to eliminate ignorance and other obscurations. (The fourth of the four dharmas is confusion dawning as wisdom, which refers to using Vajrayana techniques including mahamudra meditation to realize that all experiences are merely the display of the empty and luminous nature of mind.)—Trans.

3. The eight types of fear are fear of lions, elephants, fire, snakes, floods, chains, bandits, and flesh-eating ghosts. The sixteen types of fear are fear of

punishment by the king; the gods; illnesses from local spirits; contagious disease; famine; war; being harmed by rishis; ghosts, demons, and spirits; lightning; frost and hail; earthquakes; fire; floods; falling meteors; garudas; and bad dreams.—Trans.

4. Such as the prayer by Tertön Mingyur Dorje that begins "Emaho! The wondrous buddha Infinite Light."—Trans.

5. Nonreferential compassion arises in those who have realized the empty nature of all beings and all phenomena and focuses on sentient beings who suffer because they do not realize that nature.—Trans.

6. The five certainties are the certain place, the realm of Akanishtha; the certain body with the marks and signs of a buddha; the certain retinue of noble bodhisattvas; the certain Dharma, the Mahayana; and the certain time, until samsara has been emptied.—Trans.

GLOSSARY

✦ ✦ ✦

afflictions (Skt. klesha) The mental events of desire, aversion, ignorance, pride, stinginess, envy, and so forth, that motivate harmful actions that perpetuate samsaric suffering.

aggregates, five (Skt. skandha) The five categories of physical form and mental events that we grasp at as being a single self or as belonging to a self. The five are form, feeling, conception, formation, and consciousness.

Amitabha The buddha of the pure realm of Sukhavati, who made the aspiration that ordinary beings would be able to take rebirth in that realm.

Avalokiteshvara (Tib. Chenrezig) A bodhisattva who is the embodiment of the compassion of all the buddhas.

bardo (Tib.) The period between death and the next rebirth when the consciousness of the deceased individual experiences various appearances that occur due to past karma.

common preliminaries See **preliminaries**.

dharmakaya See **kayas**.

Dzogchen (Tib.) Literally, Great Perfection. A meditation practice for looking at the nature of the mind, primarily taught in the Nyingma tradition of Tibetan Buddhism.

Foundation Vehicle The initial teachings given by the Buddha to his disciples, which emphasize self-discipline and the lack of an individual self.

four thoughts that turn the mind See **preliminaries**.

Green Tara One of the forms of Tara, a buddha who made the vow to always appear in a female form. Green Tara's main activity is to remove obstacles and to protect beings from fear.

insight meditation (Skt. vipashyana) Meditation on the true nature of phenomena.

kayas (Skt.) The bodies of a buddha. The first is the *dharmakaya,* or body of qualities, which is the qualities of a buddha's wisdom, love, and power. As its essence is wisdom, it is perceived only by the buddhas. Since others cannot perceive the dharmakaya, buddhas manifest two kinds of form kayas. The *sambhogakaya,* or enjoyment body, is visible only to those beings on high bodhisattva levels who have pure perception. The *nirmanakaya,* or emanation body, can be perceived by ordinary beings with impure perception. An example of a nirmanakaya would be the Shakyamuni Buddha; an example of a sambhogakaya would be Avalokiteshvara. Sometimes the buddhas are also described as having a fourth kaya, the *svabhavikakaya,* or essence body, which is described alternately as the union of the three kayas or as their empty nature.

lojong (Tib.) Literally, mind training. A set of practices for training the mind to develop bodhichitta and decrease ego-clinging.

mahamudra (Skt.) Literally, great seal. A method of meditating directly on the nature of mind from the Indian tradition. In Tibet it became a major practice of the Kagyu lineage.

mahasiddha (Skt.) A great master of meditation who has attained high levels of accomplishment.

Mahayana (Skt.) Literally, Great Vehicle. The second set of teachings given by the Buddha, which emphasize compassion and the lack of a self in phenomena.

Medicine Buddha A buddha who made the aspiration in a previous life to be able to free sentient beings from the suffering of illness and thus gained that ability upon awakening to buddhahood.

Middle Way A Mahayana philosophical school that teaches the empty nature of phenomena using logical means.

nirmanakaya See **kayas.**

paramitas, six (Skt.) Transcendent generosity, discipline, patience, diligence, meditation, and wisdom (or prajna). *Paramita* means "gone beyond." These qualities are so called because they transcend ordinary, worldly generosity and so forth.

prajnaparamita See **paramitas, six.**

precious human life A human birth with the eight leisures and ten resources that allow the practice of Dharma. The eight leisures are states of freedom from conditions in which one cannot practice Dharma: not being born in the hells, as a hungry ghost, as an animal, as a barbarian, as a long-lived god, with a wrong view, where the buddha has not appeared, or with impaired faculties. The ten resources are advantages that allow Dharma practice. Five depend on oneself: being born as a human, in a central land, with full faculties, with right livelihood, and with faith in the Three Jewels. Five depend on external conditions: the Buddha's having appeared in the world and having taught the Dharma, the teachings remaining, entering the teachings, and having all the resources to practice the Dharma.

preliminaries Meditation practices that strengthen one's motivation to practice the Dharma and provide a foundation for further practice. There are two sets of preliminaries: common and special. The common preliminaries, known as the four thoughts that turn the mind, are meditations on the precious human life; death and impermanence; karma, cause, and effect; and the defects of samsara. These contemplations turn one's mind away from worldly concerns and increase the wish to practice Dharma. The special preliminaries are the four practices of refuge and prostrations, Vajrasattva meditation, mandala offering, and guru yoga. These practices purify one's being, gather the accumulations of merit and wisdom, and incorporate the lama's blessings into the student's being, thus preparing him or her for the actual practices of mahamudra and so forth.

samadhi (Skt.) Deep and stable meditation.

sambhogakaya See **kayas.**

special preliminaries See **preliminaries.**

Sukhavati (Skt.) The pure realm of the buddha Amitabha, located to the west of this universe. Because of the power of Amitabha's aspirations, ordinary sentient beings can be born in this realm if they imagine it, gather the accumulation of merit, generate bodhichitta, and make aspirations to be reborn there.

tonglen (Tib.) Literally, sending and taking. A lojong practice designed to decrease ego-clinging and increase altruism. In this practice, one imagines giving all one's own happiness and its causes to others and taking all of their suffering and its causes upon oneself.

torma (Tib.) A sculpted cake made of edible substances that is used as an offering, especially in Vajrayana ritual practice.

tranquillity meditation (Skt. shamatha) Meditation that is primarily intended to increase the stability of mind so that one can rest without distraction.

Vajrapani A great bodhisattva dwelling in the pure realm of Sukhavati.

Vajrayana (Skt.) A branch of the Mahayana that uses many different techniques such as mantra, visualization, ritual, and looking directly at the nature of the mind in order to bring results quickly.

yidam (Tib.) A meditational deity.

Printed in the United States
by Baker & Taylor Publisher Services